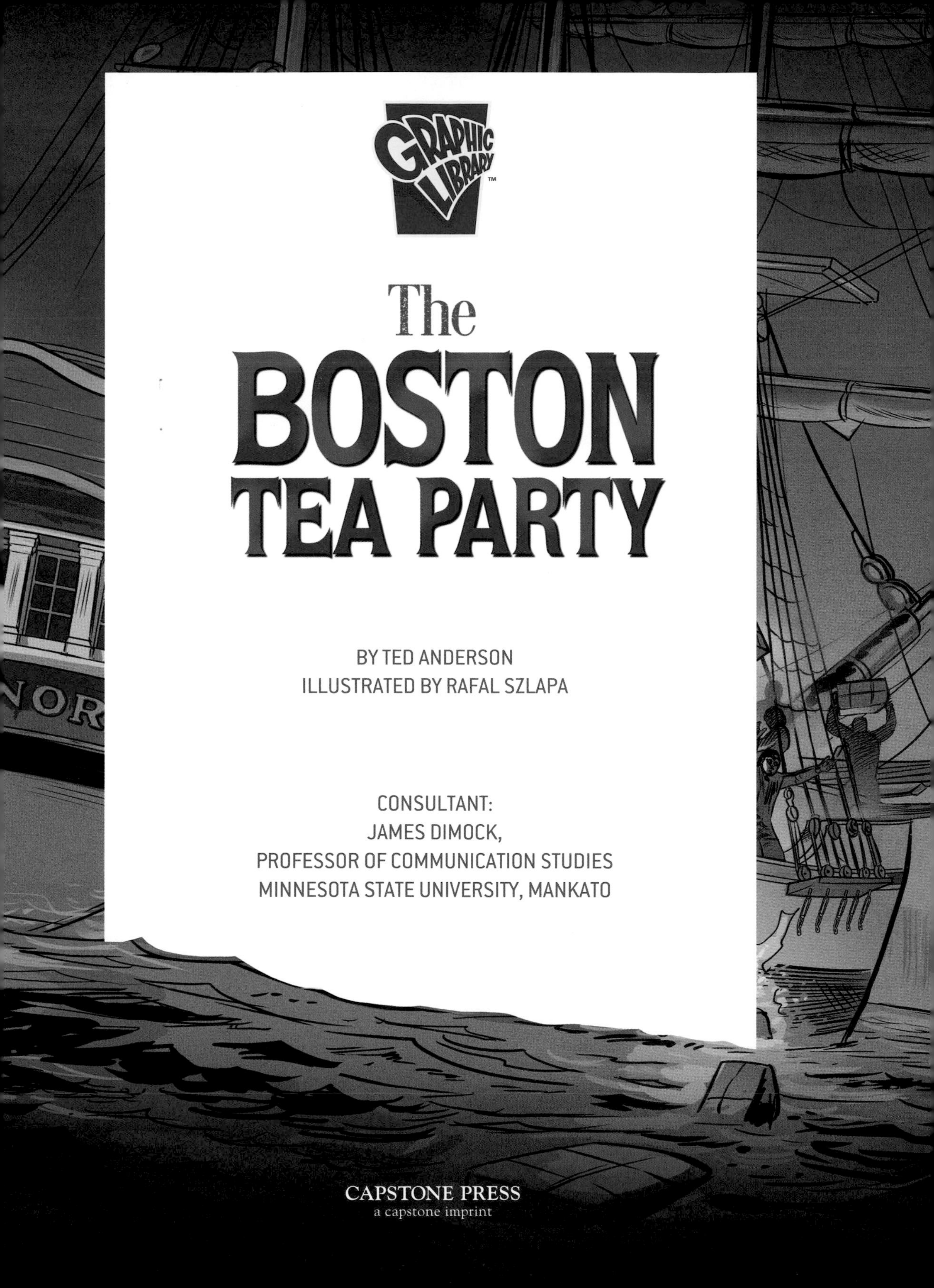

The BOSTON TEA PARTY

BY TED ANDERSON
ILLUSTRATED BY RAFAL SZLAPA

CONSULTANT:
JAMES DIMOCK,
PROFESSOR OF COMMUNICATION STUDIES
MINNESOTA STATE UNIVERSITY, MANKATO

CAPSTONE PRESS
a capstone imprint

Graphic Library is published by Capstone Press, an imprint of Capstone.
1710 Roe Crest Drive
North Mankato, Minnesota 56003
www.capstonepub.com

Library of Congress Cataloging-in-Publication Data is available on the Library of Congress website.

ISBN: 978-1-4966-8110-2 (library binding)
ISBN: 978-1-4966-8687-9 (paperback)
ISBN: 978-1-4966-8125-6 (eBook PDF)

Summary: By December 1773, American colonists had grown increasingly frustrated. Among their complaints was that the British government had imposed a tea tax on colonists. The Americans objected because it was taxation without representation—that is, they had no say in who was elected to the British Parliament. As tensions grew, plans formed to protest the tax by tossing hundreds of containers of tea into Boston Harbor. One of the first acts of protest in America, the Boston Tea Party helped spark America's fight for independence.

Editorial Credits
Editor: Julie Gassman; Designer: Tracy McCabe;
Media Researcher: Eric Gohl; Production Specialist: Laura Manthe

Design Elements
Shutterstock: DMG Vision, 30–32 (background)

All internet sites appearing in back matter were available and accurate when this book was sent to press.

Printed in the United States of America.
PA117

TABLE OF CONTENTS

TRADES AND TAXES

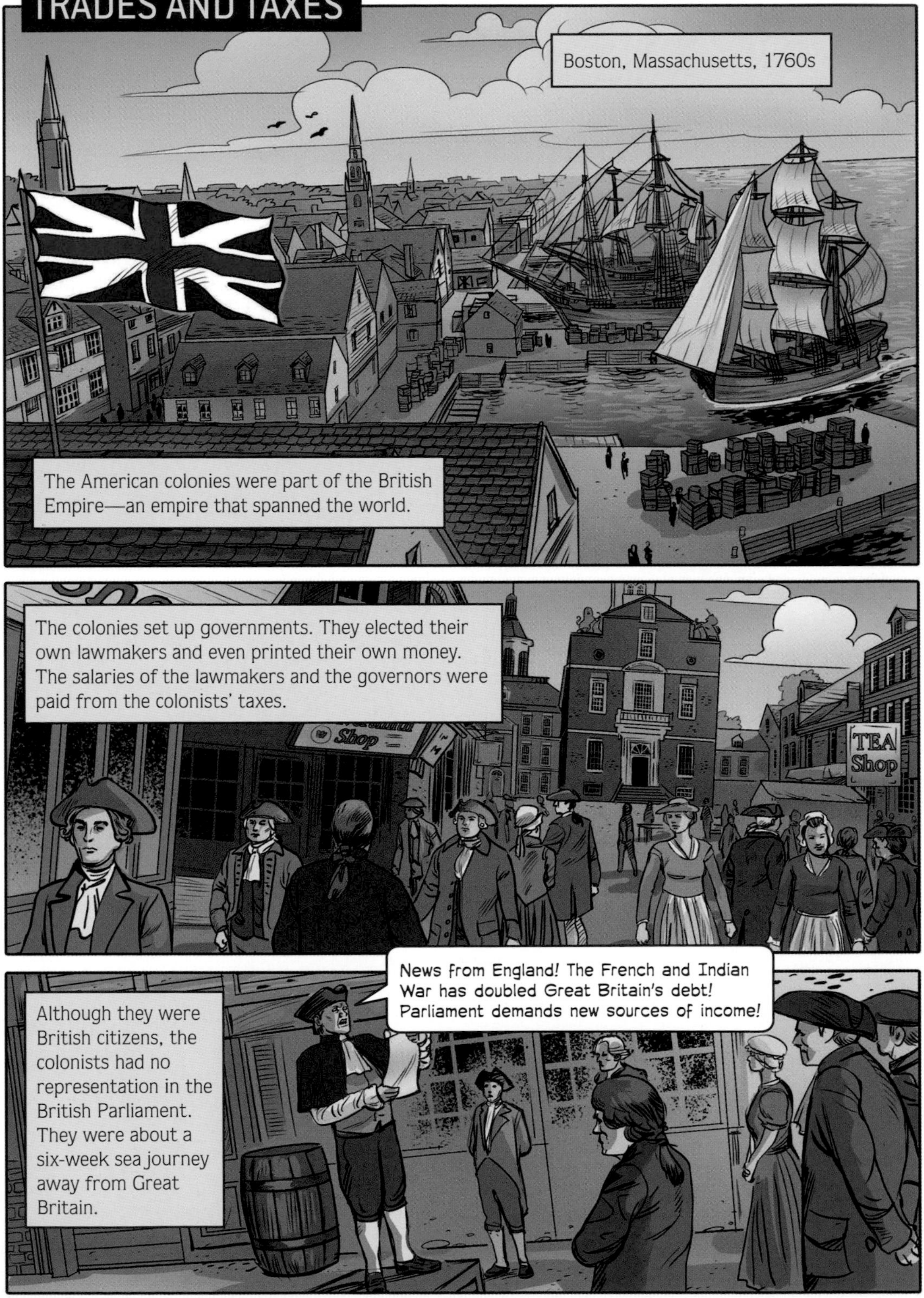

Boston, Massachusetts, 1760s
The American colonies were part of the British Empire—an empire that spanned the world.
The colonies set up governments. They elected their own lawmakers and even printed their own money. The salaries of the lawmakers and the governors were paid from the colonists' taxes.
Shop
TEA Shop
Although they were British citizens, the colonists had no representation in the British Parliament. They were about a six-week sea journey away from Great Britain.
News from England! The French and Indian War has doubled Great Britain's debt! Parliament demands new sources of income!

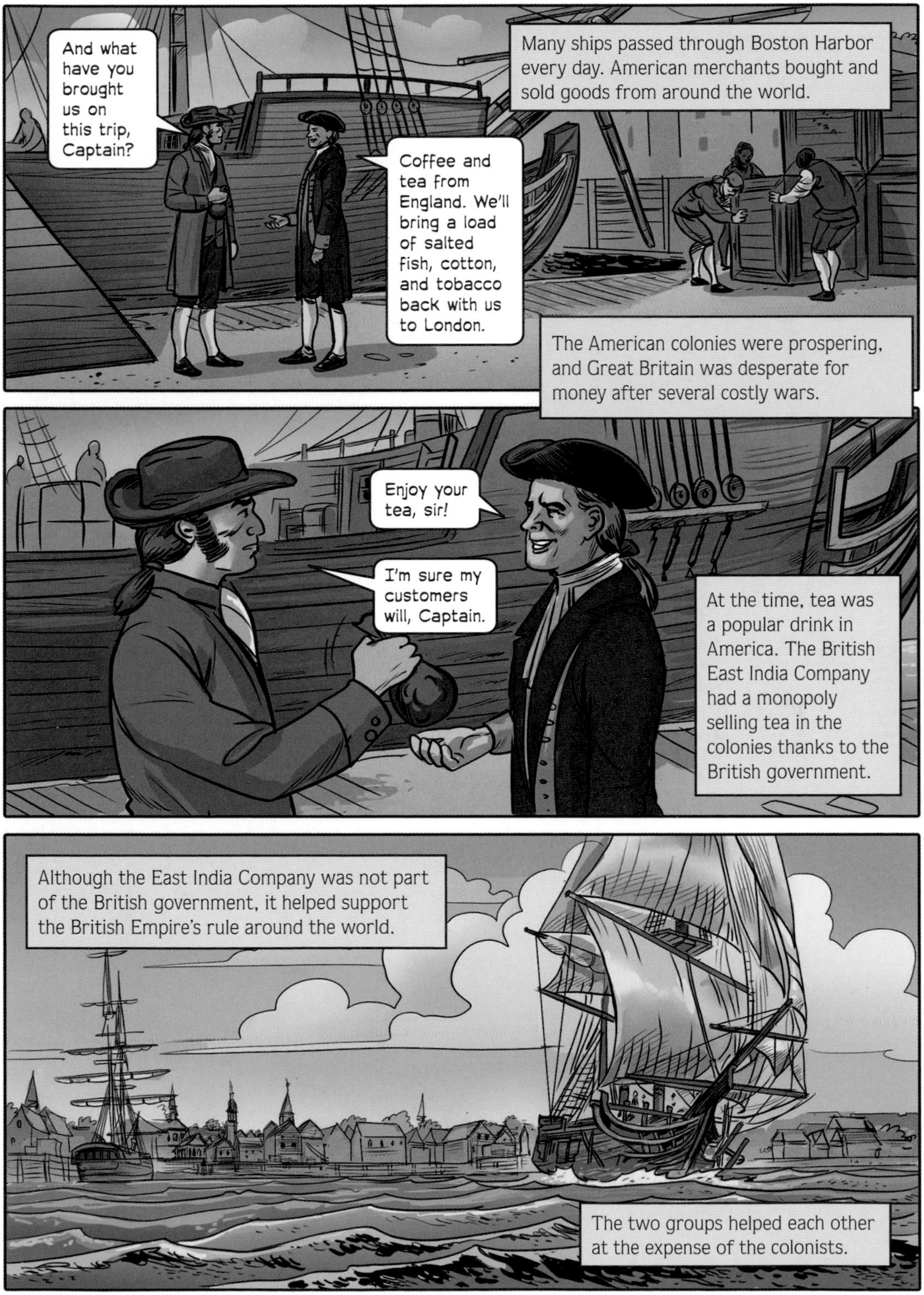
And what have you brought us on this trip, Captain?
Coffee and tea from England. We'll bring a load of salted fish, cotton, and tobacco back with us to London.
Many ships passed through Boston Harbor every day. American merchants bought and sold goods from around the world.
The American colonies were prospering, and Great Britain was desperate for money after several costly wars.
Enjoy your tea, sir!
I'm sure my customers will, Captain.
At the time, tea was a popular drink in America. The British East India Company had a monopoly selling tea in the colonies thanks to the British government.
Although the East India Company was not part of the British government, it helped support the British Empire's rule around the world.
The two groups helped each other at the expense of the colonists.

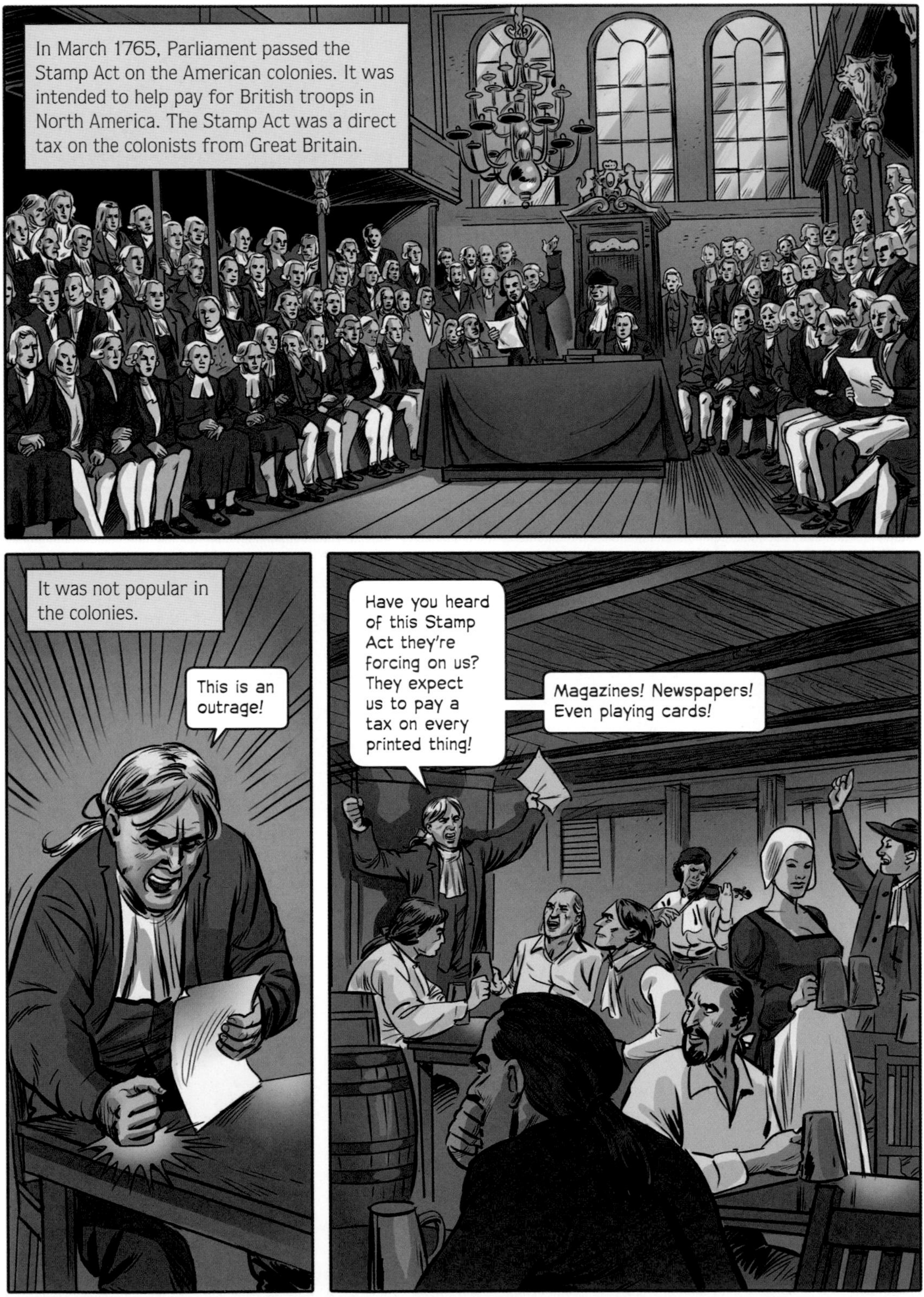
In March 1765, Parliament passed the Stamp Act on the American colonies. It was intended to help pay for British troops in North America. The Stamp Act was a direct tax on the colonists from Great Britain.
It was not popular in the colonies.
This is an outrage!
Have you heard of this Stamp Act they're forcing on us? They expect us to pay a tax on every printed thing!
Magazines! Newspapers! Even playing cards!

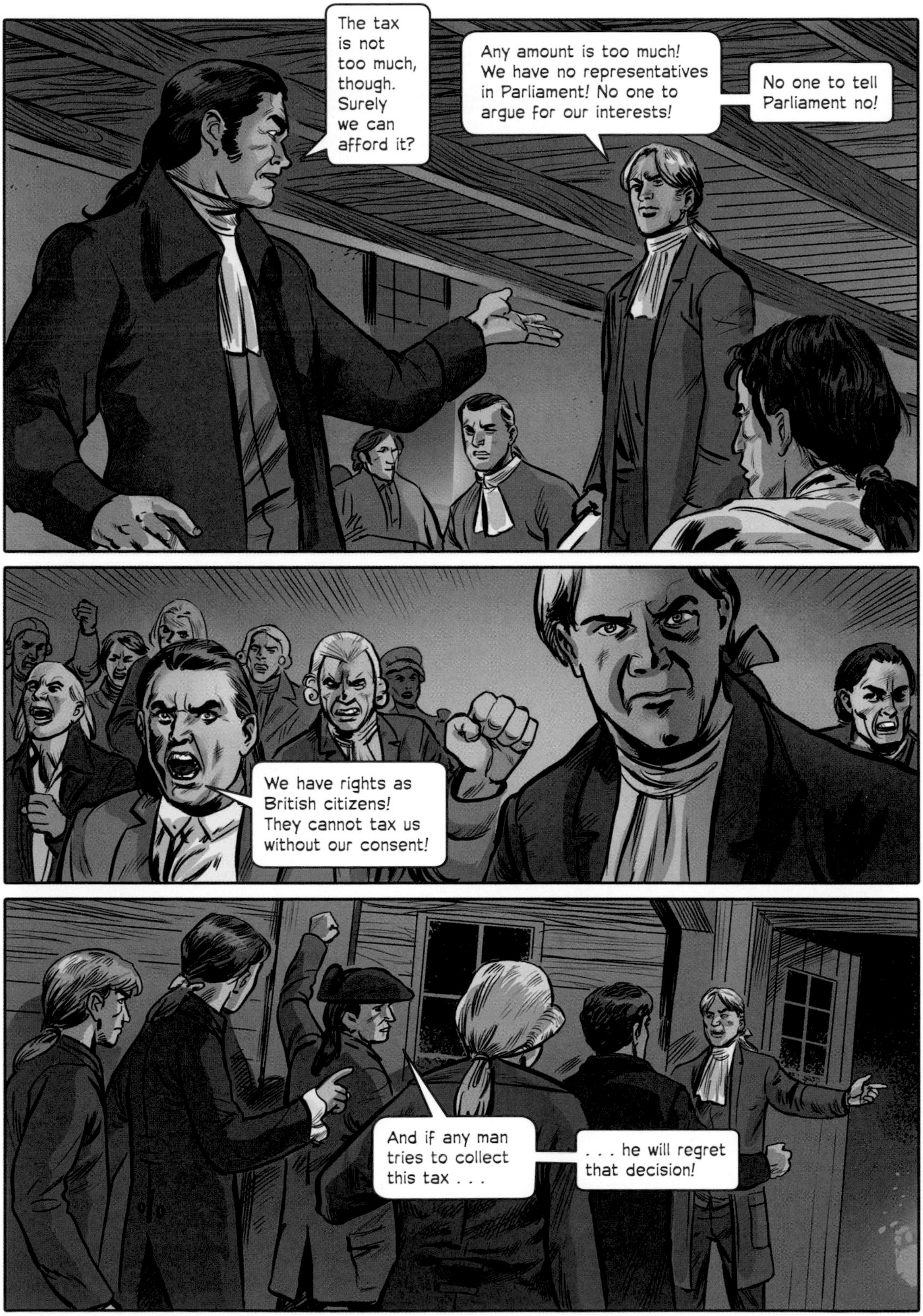
The tax is not too much, though. Surely we can afford it?
Any amount is too much! We have no representatives in Parliament! No one to argue for our interests!
No one to tell Parliament no!
We have rights as British citizens! They cannot tax us without our consent!
And if any man tries to collect this tax . . .
. . . he will regret that decision!

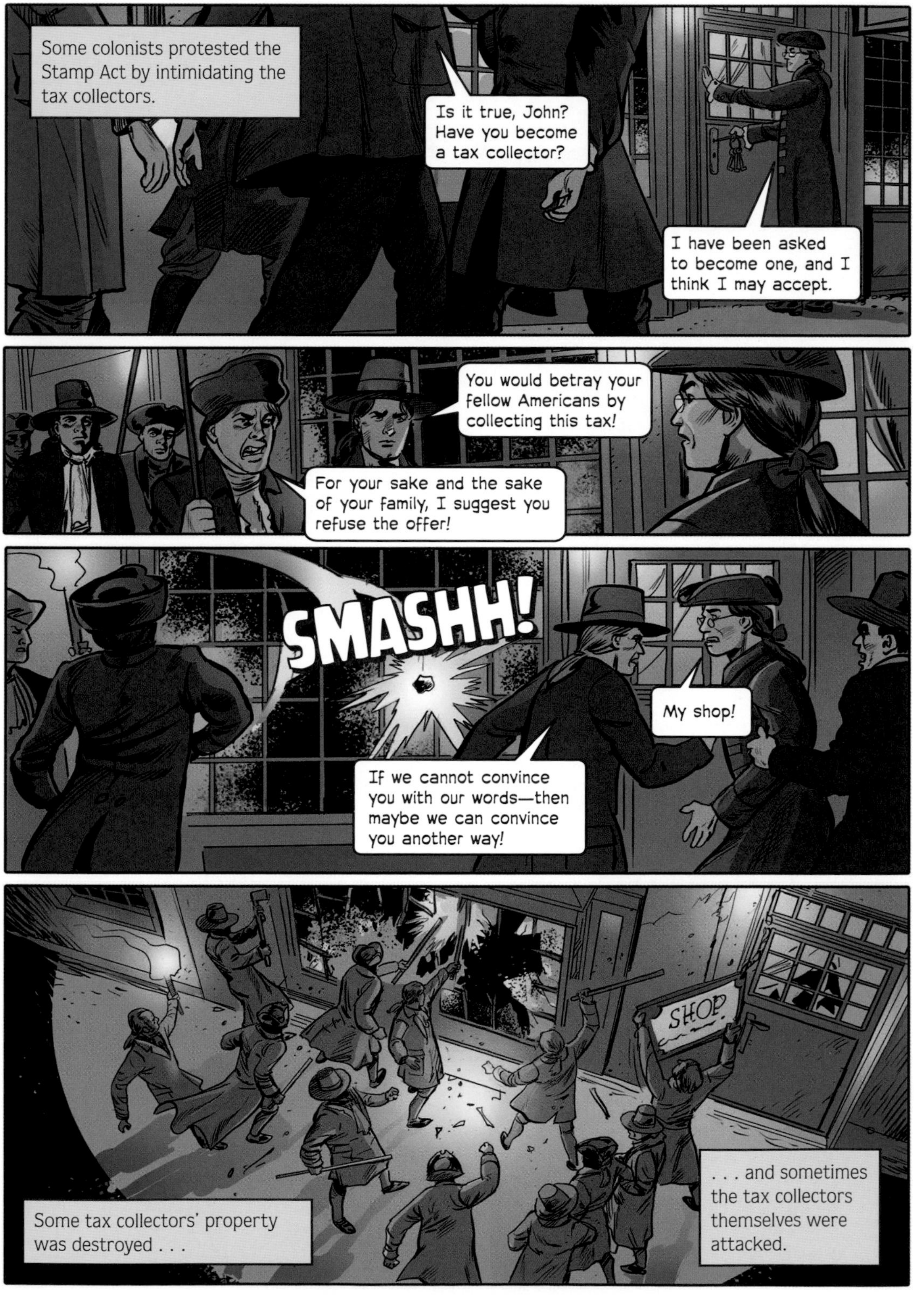
Some colonists protested the Stamp Act by intimidating the tax collectors.
Is it true, John? Have you become a tax collector?
I have been asked to become one, and I think I may accept.
You would betray your fellow Americans by collecting this tax!
For your sake and the sake of your family, I suggest you refuse the offer!
SMASHH!
My shop!
If we cannot convince you with our words—then maybe we can convince you another way!
SHOP
Some tax collectors' property was destroyed . . .
. . . and sometimes the tax collectors themselves were attacked.

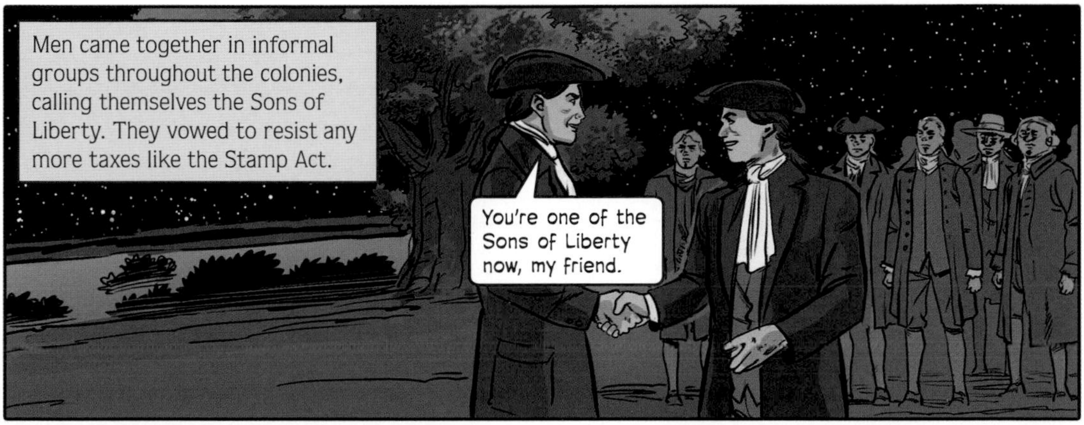
Men came together in informal groups throughout the colonies, calling themselves the Sons of Liberty. They vowed to resist any more taxes like the Stamp Act.
You're one of the Sons of Liberty now, my friend.

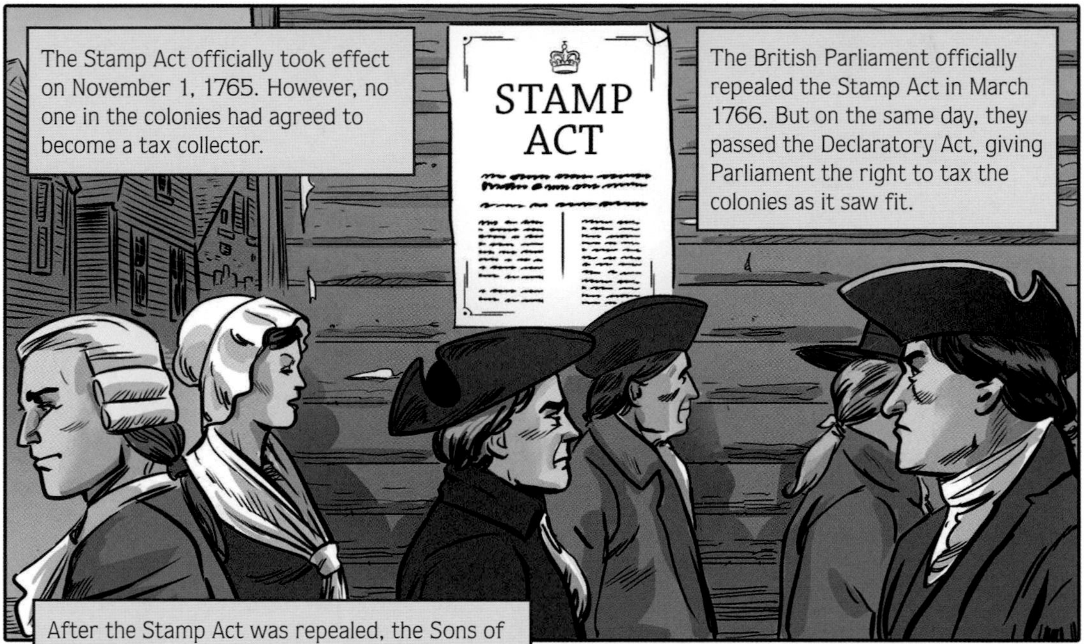
The Stamp Act officially took effect on November 1, 1765. However, no one in the colonies had agreed to become a tax collector.
STAMP ACT
The British Parliament officially repealed the Stamp Act in March 1766. But on the same day, they passed the Declaratory Act, giving Parliament the right to tax the colonies as it saw fit.

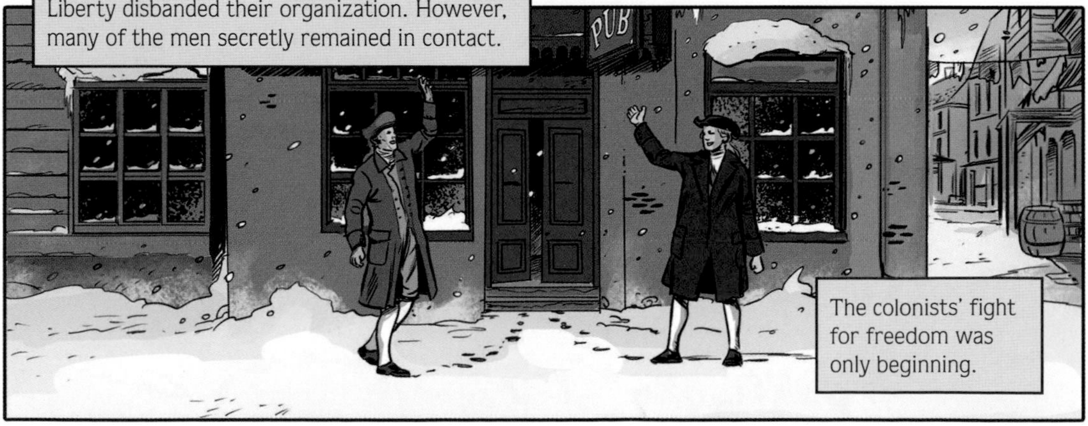
After the Stamp Act was repealed, the Sons of Liberty disbanded their organization. However, many of the men secretly remained in contact.
PUB
The colonists' fight for freedom was only beginning.

THE TOWNSHEND ACTS

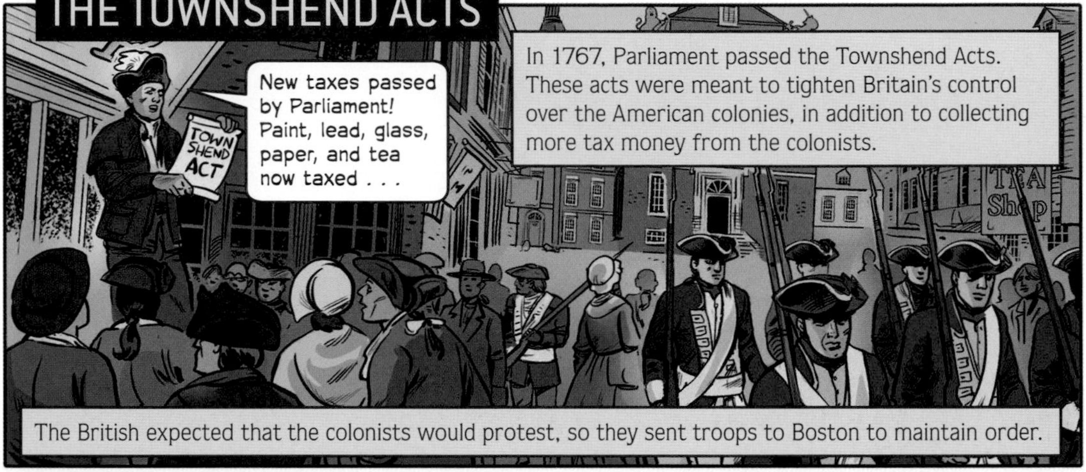
In 1767, Parliament passed the Townshend Acts. These acts were meant to tighten Britain's control over the American colonies, in addition to collecting more tax money from the colonists.
New taxes passed by Parliament! Paint, lead, glass, paper, and tea now taxed . . .
TOWNSHEND ACT
The British expected that the colonists would protest, so they sent troops to Boston to maintain order.

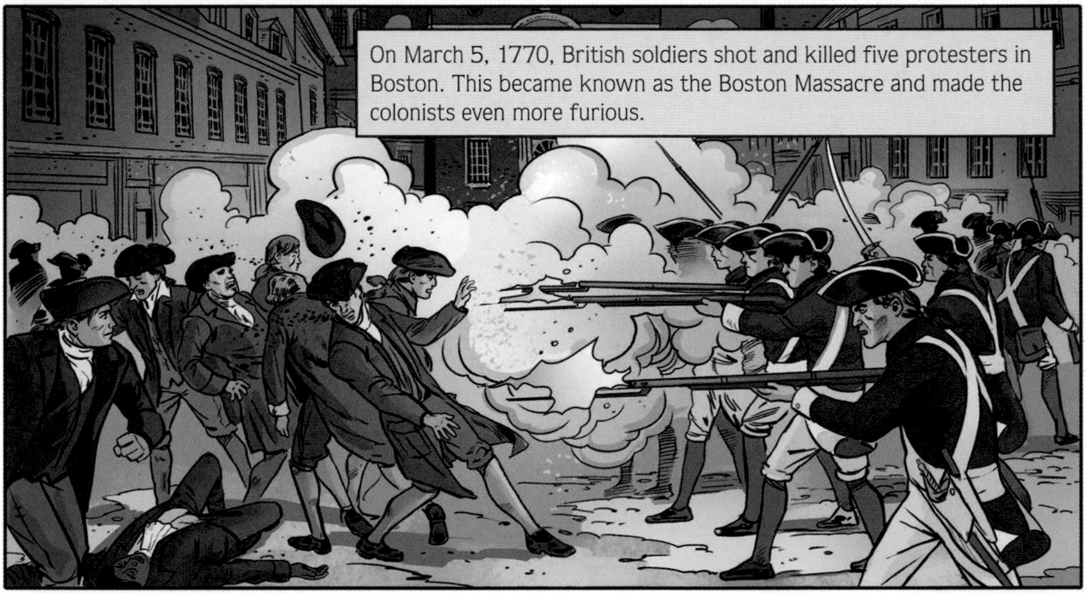
On March 5, 1770, British soldiers shot and killed five protesters in Boston. This became known as the Boston Massacre and made the colonists even more furious.

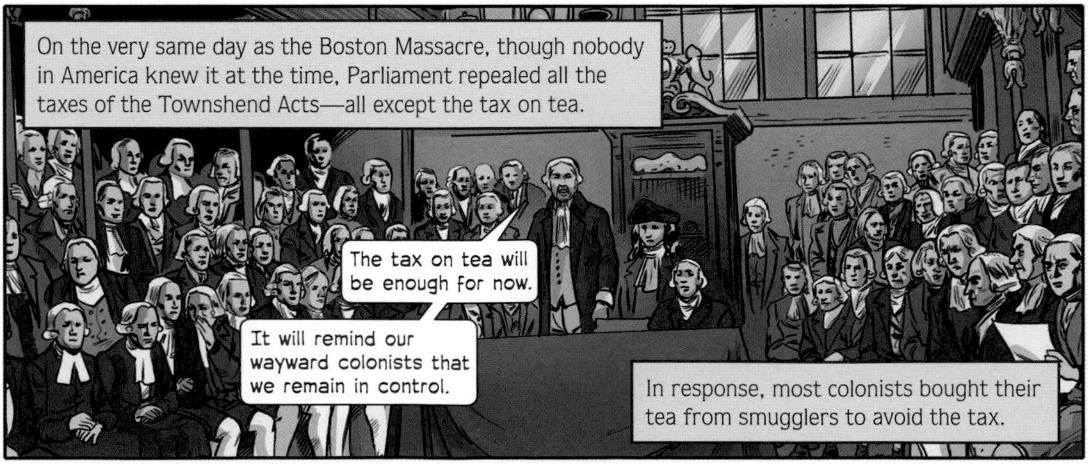
On the very same day as the Boston Massacre, though nobody in America knew it at the time, Parliament repealed all the taxes of the Townshend Acts—all except the tax on tea.
The tax on tea will be enough for now.
It will remind our wayward colonists that we remain in control.
In response, most colonists bought their tea from smugglers to avoid the tax.

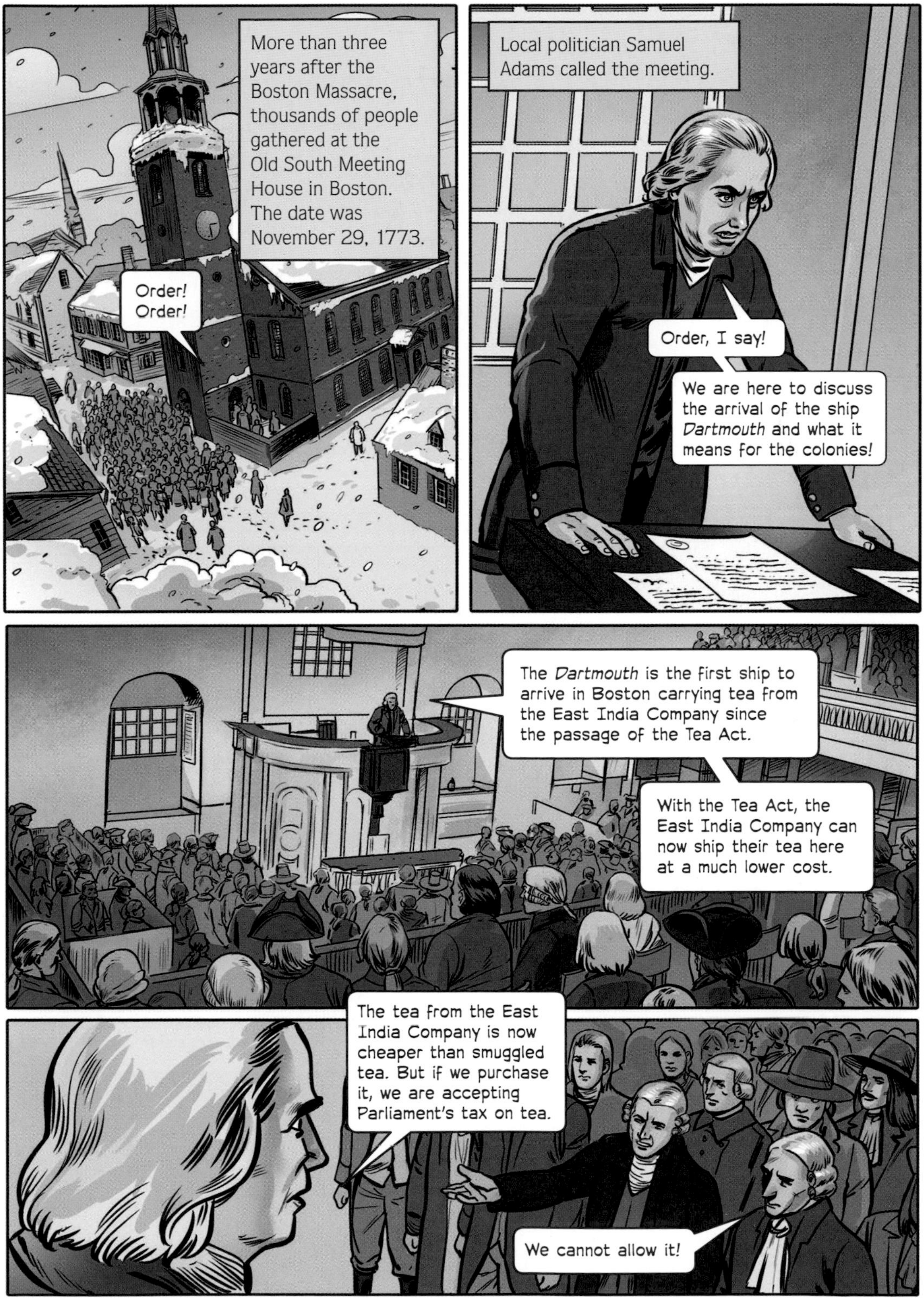
More than three years after the Boston Massacre, thousands of people gathered at the Old South Meeting House in Boston. The date was November 29, 1773.
Order! Order!
Local politician Samuel Adams called the meeting.
Order, I say!
We are here to discuss the arrival of the ship *Dartmouth* and what it means for the colonies!
The *Dartmouth* is the first ship to arrive in Boston carrying tea from the East India Company since the passage of the Tea Act.
With the Tea Act, the East India Company can now ship their tea here at a much lower cost.
The tea from the East India Company is now cheaper than smuggled tea. But if we purchase it, we are accepting Parliament's tax on tea.
We cannot allow it!

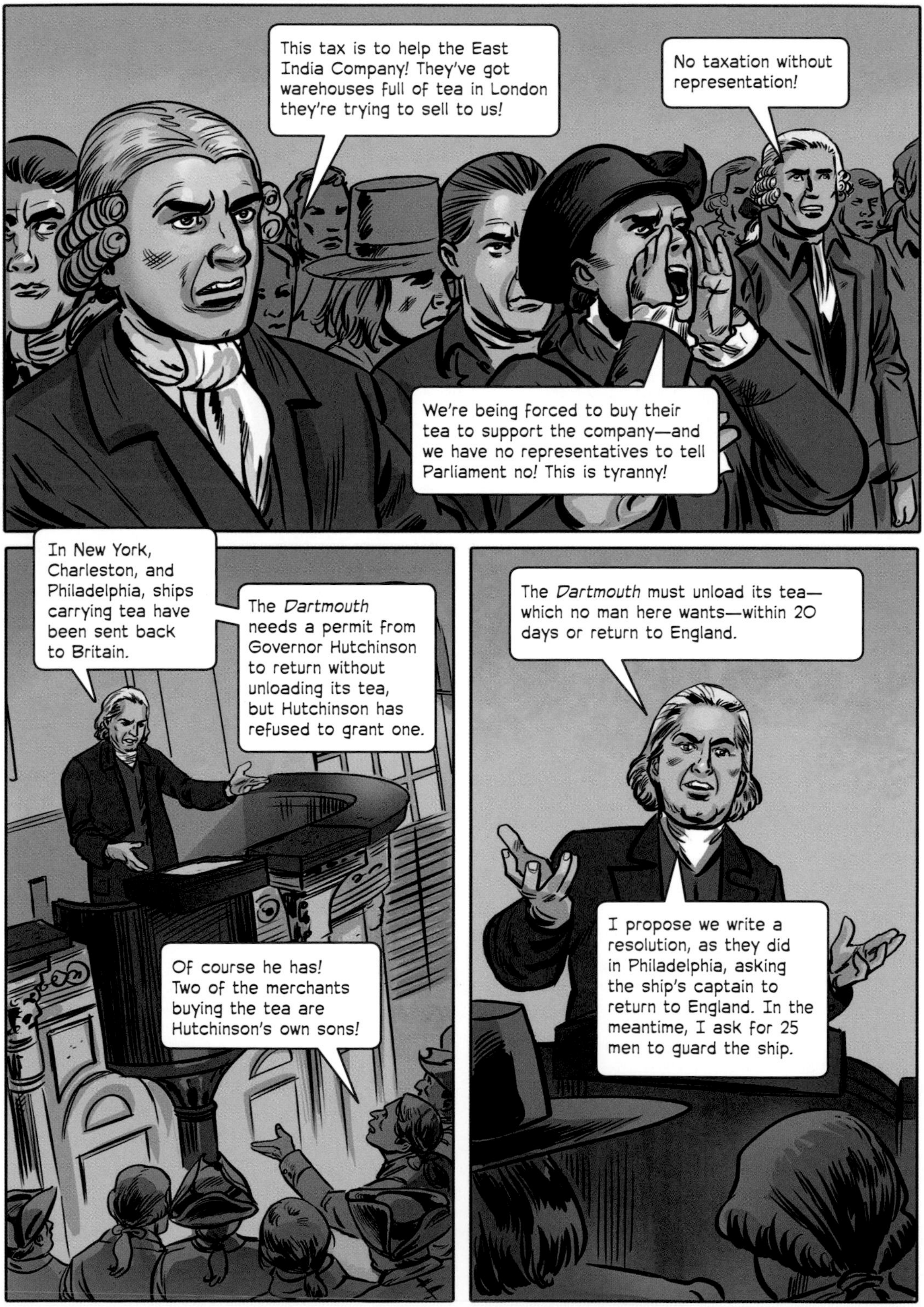
This tax is to help the East India Company! They've got warehouses full of tea in London they're trying to sell to us!
No taxation without representation!
We're being forced to buy their tea to support the company—and we have no representatives to tell Parliament no! This is tyranny!
In New York, Charleston, and Philadelphia, ships carrying tea have been sent back to Britain.
The *Dartmouth* needs a permit from Governor Hutchinson to return without unloading its tea, but Hutchinson has refused to grant one.
Of course he has! Two of the merchants buying the tea are Hutchinson's own sons!
The *Dartmouth* must unload its tea—which no man here wants—within 20 days or return to England.
I propose we write a resolution, as they did in Philadelphia, asking the ship's captain to return to England. In the meantime, I ask for 25 men to guard the ship.

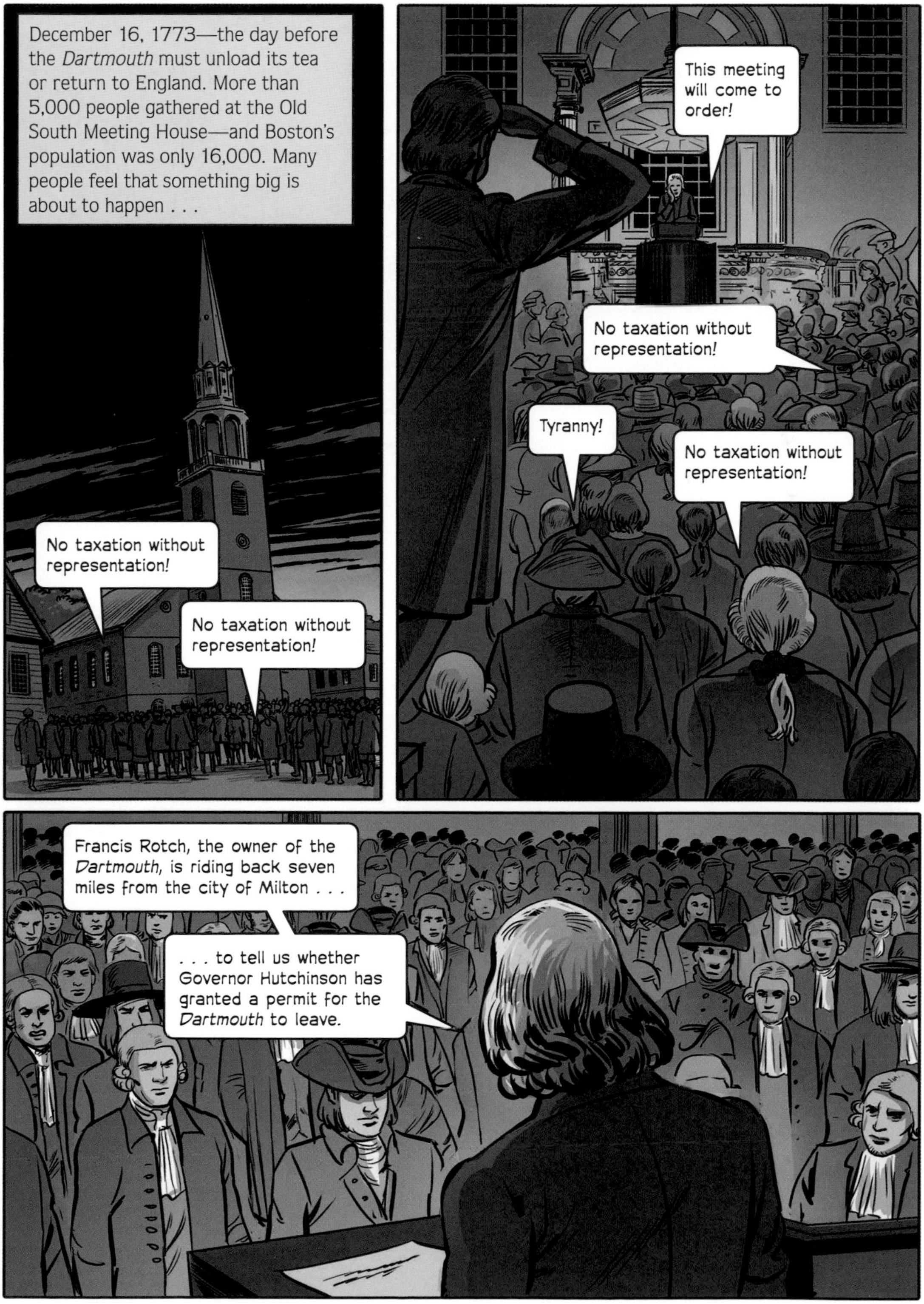
December 16, 1773—the day before the *Dartmouth* must unload its tea or return to England. More than 5,000 people gathered at the Old South Meeting House—and Boston's population was only 16,000. Many people feel that something big is about to happen . . .
No taxation without representation!
No taxation without representation!
This meeting will come to order!
No taxation without representation!
Tyranny!
No taxation without representation!
Francis Rotch, the owner of the *Dartmouth*, is riding back seven miles from the city of Milton . . .
. . . to tell us whether Governor Hutchinson has granted a permit for the *Dartmouth* to leave.

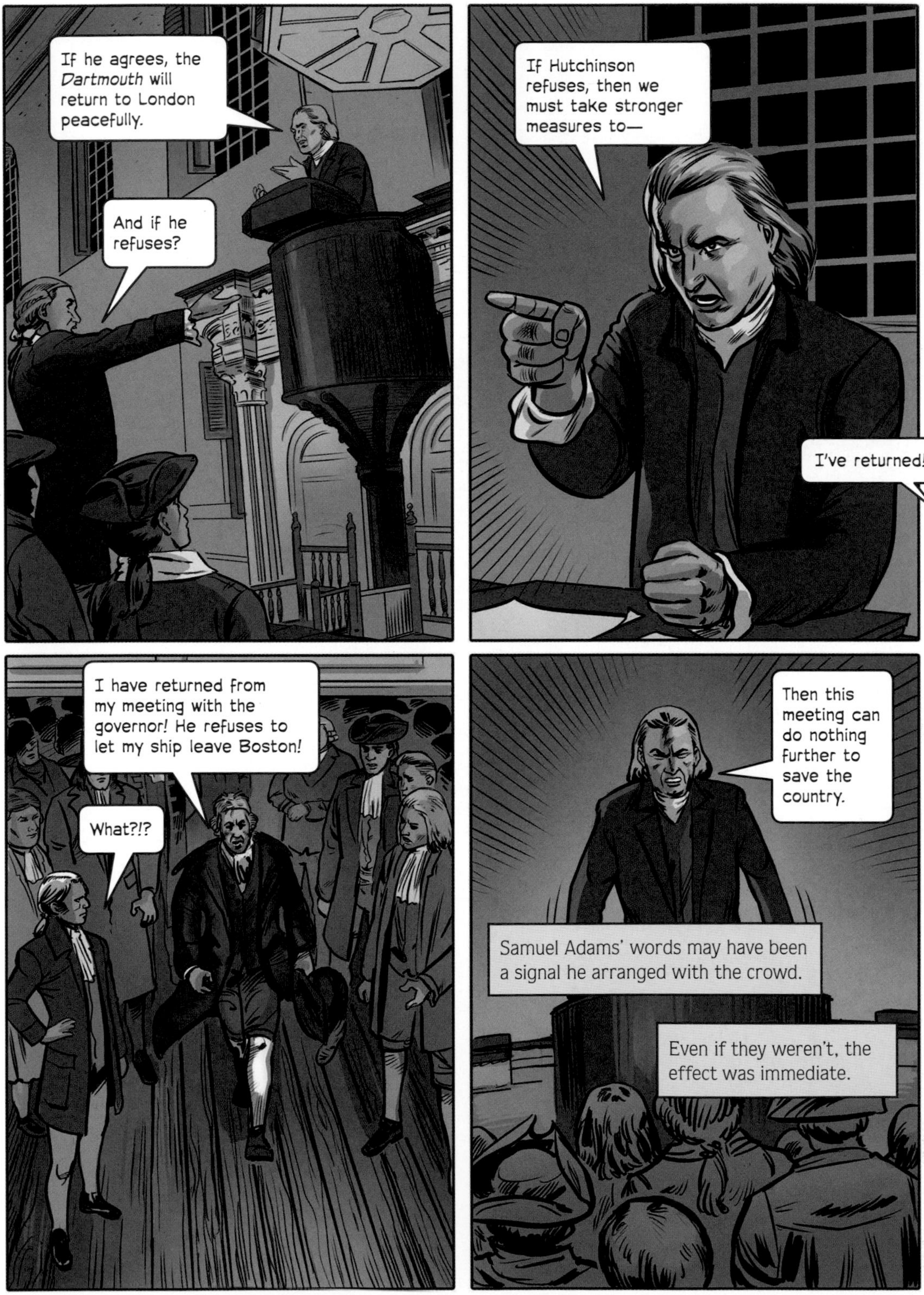
If he agrees, the *Dartmouth* will return to London peacefully.
And if he refuses?
If Hutchinson refuses, then we must take stronger measures to—
I've returned!
I have returned from my meeting with the governor! He refuses to let my ship leave Boston!
What?!?
Then this meeting can do nothing further to save the country.
Samuel Adams' words may have been a signal he arranged with the crowd.
Even if they weren't, the effect was immediate.

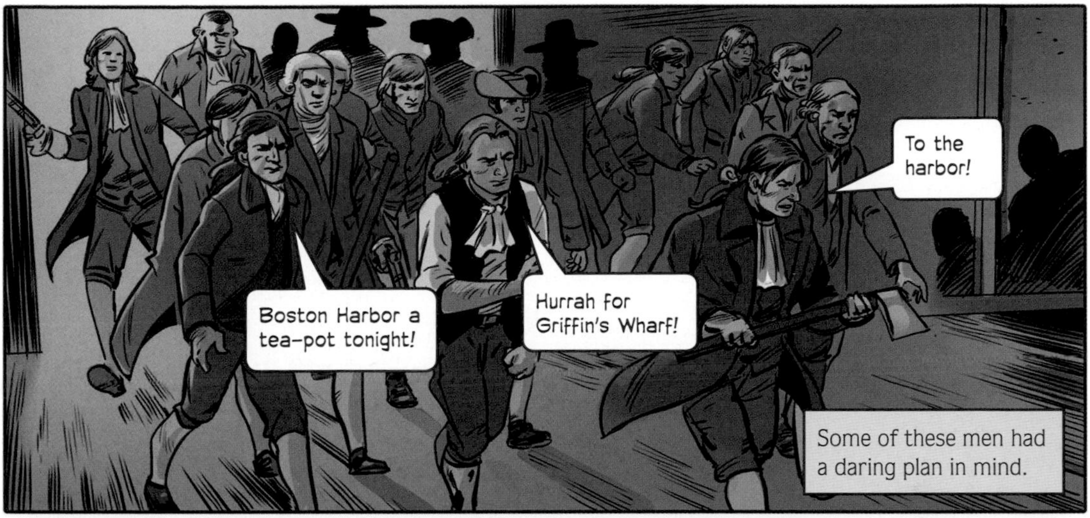
To the harbor!
Boston Harbor a tea-pot tonight!
Hurrah for Griffin's Wharf!
Some of these men had a daring plan in mind.

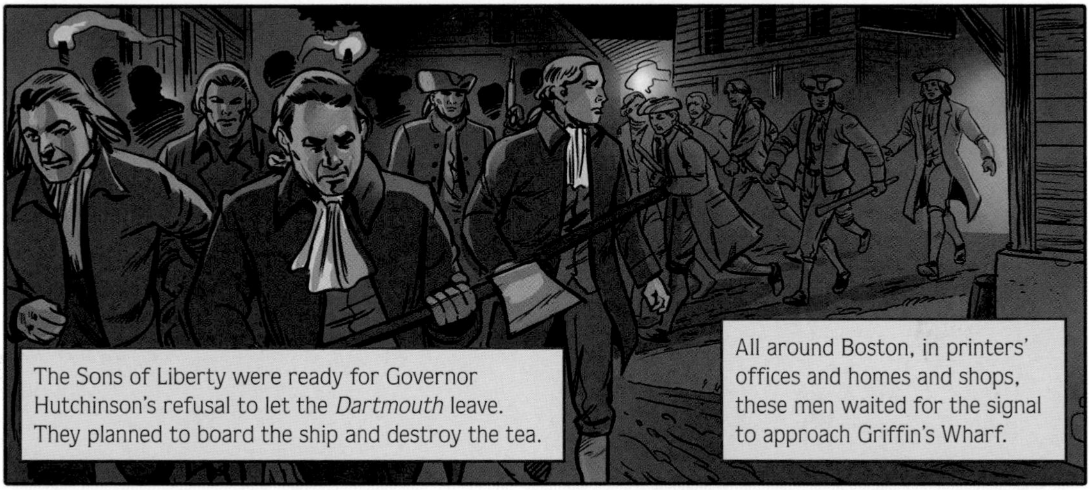
The Sons of Liberty were ready for Governor Hutchinson's refusal to let the *Dartmouth* leave. They planned to board the ship and destroy the tea.
All around Boston, in printers' offices and homes and shops, these men waited for the signal to approach Griffin's Wharf.

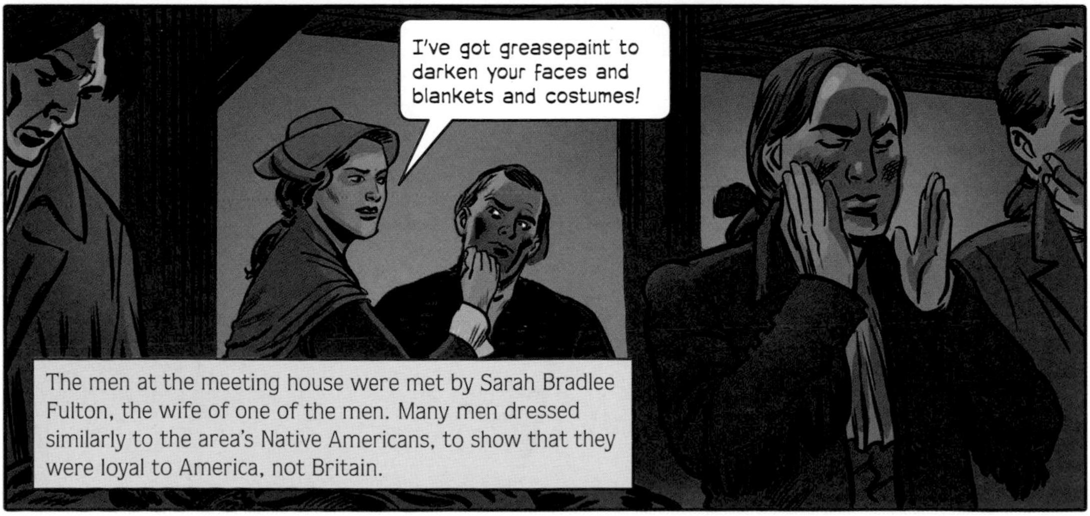
I've got greasepaint to darken your faces and blankets and costumes!
The men at the meeting house were met by Sarah Bradlee Fulton, the wife of one of the men. Many men dressed similarly to the area's Native Americans, to show that they were loyal to America, not Britain.

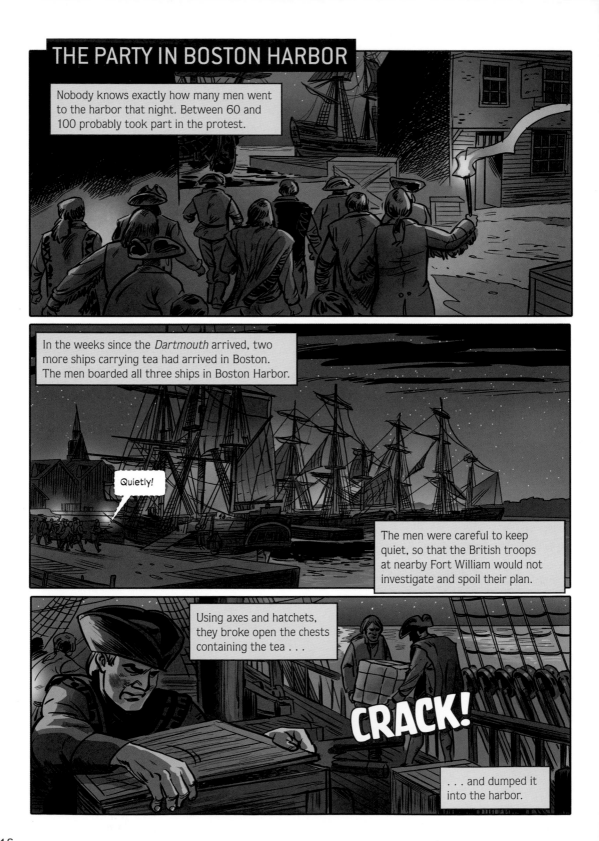

THE PARTY IN BOSTON HARBOR

Nobody knows exactly how many men went to the harbor that night. Between 60 and 100 probably took part in the protest.

In the weeks since the *Dartmouth* arrived, two more ships carrying tea had arrived in Boston. The men boarded all three ships in Boston Harbor.

Quietly!

The men were careful to keep quiet, so that the British troops at nearby Fort William would not investigate and spoil their plan.

Using axes and hatchets, they broke open the chests containing the tea . . .

CRACK!

. . . and dumped it into the harbor.

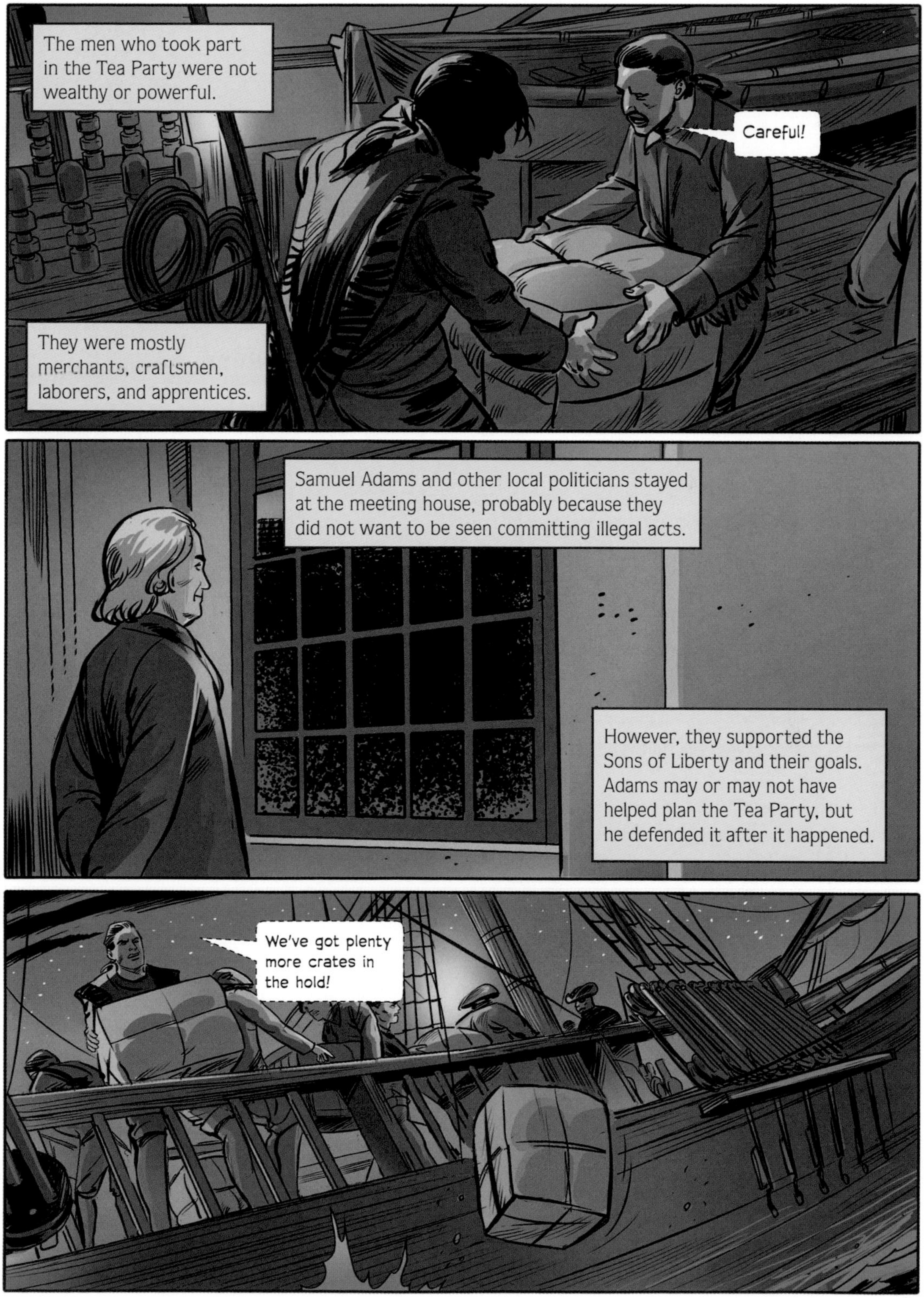
The men who took part in the Tea Party were not wealthy or powerful.
Careful!
They were mostly merchants, craftsmen, laborers, and apprentices.
Samuel Adams and other local politicians stayed at the meeting house, probably because they did not want to be seen committing illegal acts.
However, they supported the Sons of Liberty and their goals. Adams may or may not have helped plan the Tea Party, but he defended it after it happened.
We've got plenty more crates in the hold!

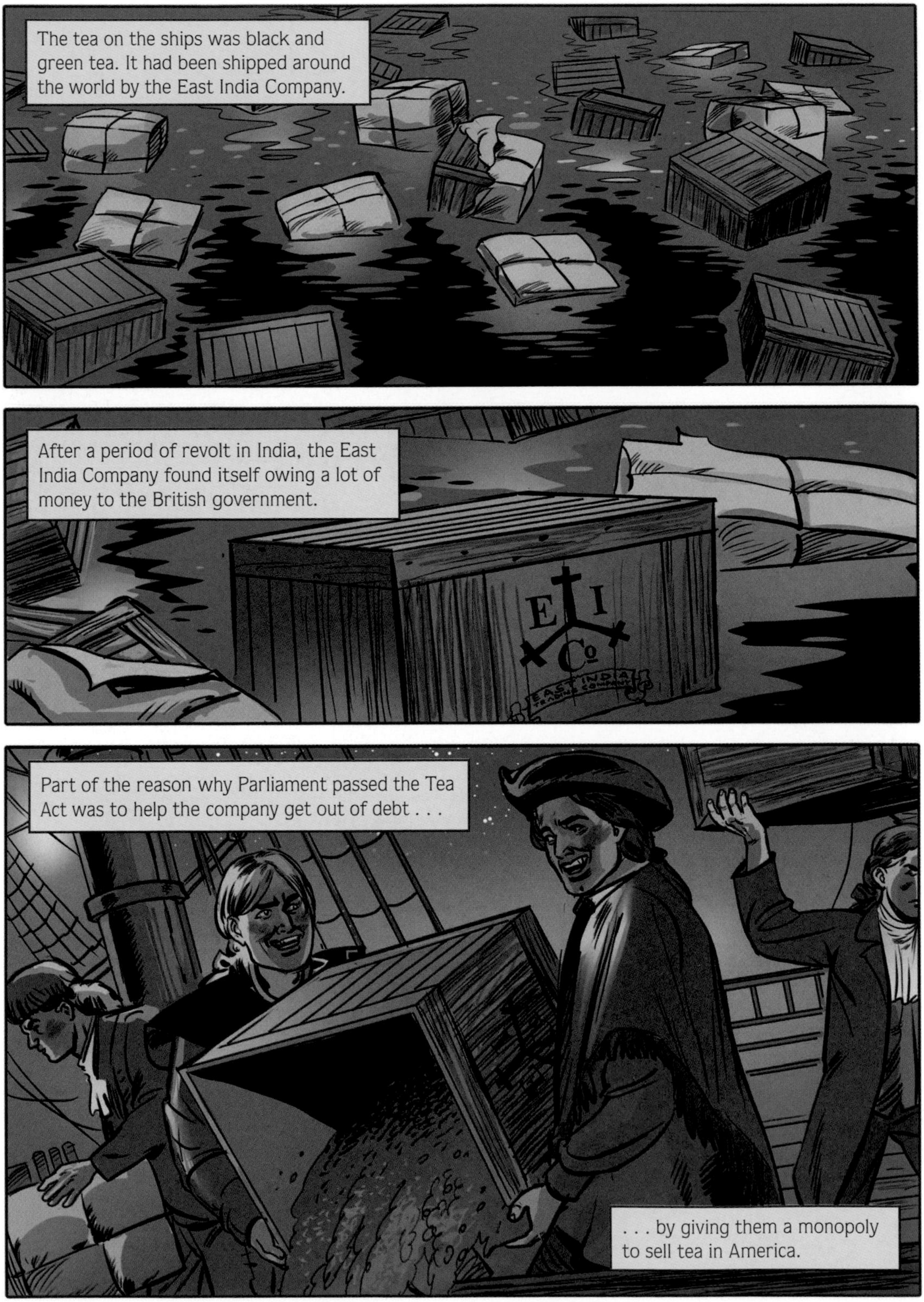
The tea on the ships was black and green tea. It had been shipped around the world by the East India Company.
After a period of revolt in India, the East India Company found itself owing a lot of money to the British government.
Part of the reason why Parliament passed the Tea Act was to help the company get out of debt . . .
. . . by giving them a monopoly to sell tea in America.

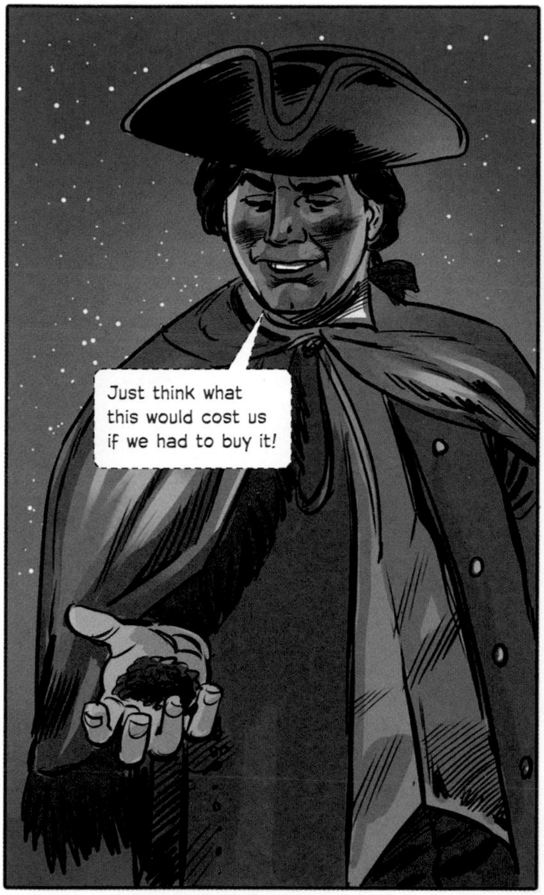
Just think what this would cost us if we had to buy it!

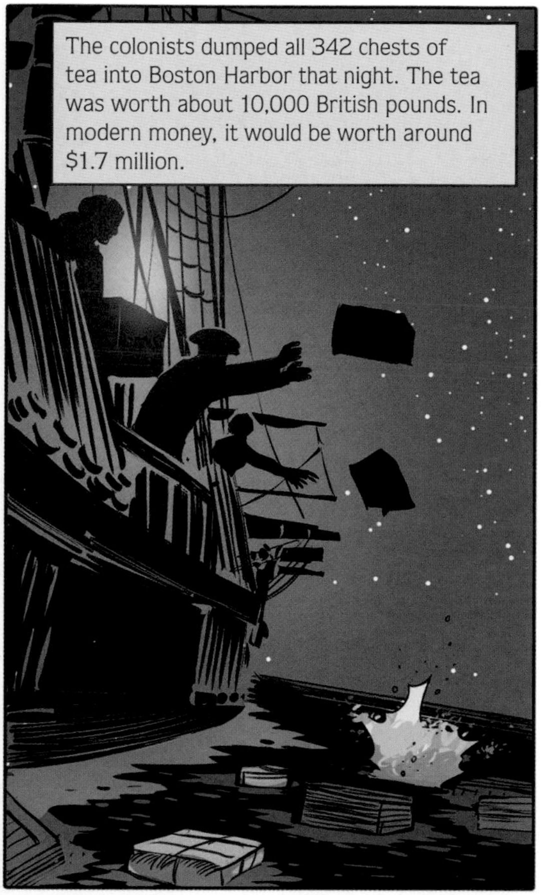
The colonists dumped all 342 chests of tea into Boston Harbor that night. The tea was worth about 10,000 British pounds. In modern money, it would be worth around $1.7 million.

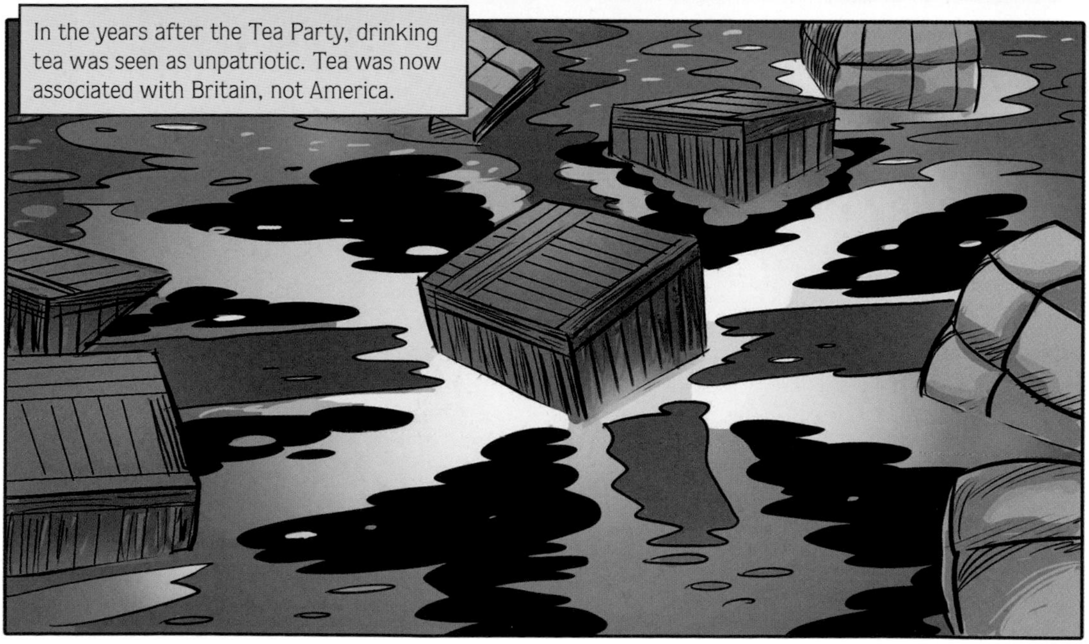
In the years after the Tea Party, drinking tea was seen as unpatriotic. Tea was now associated with Britain, not America.

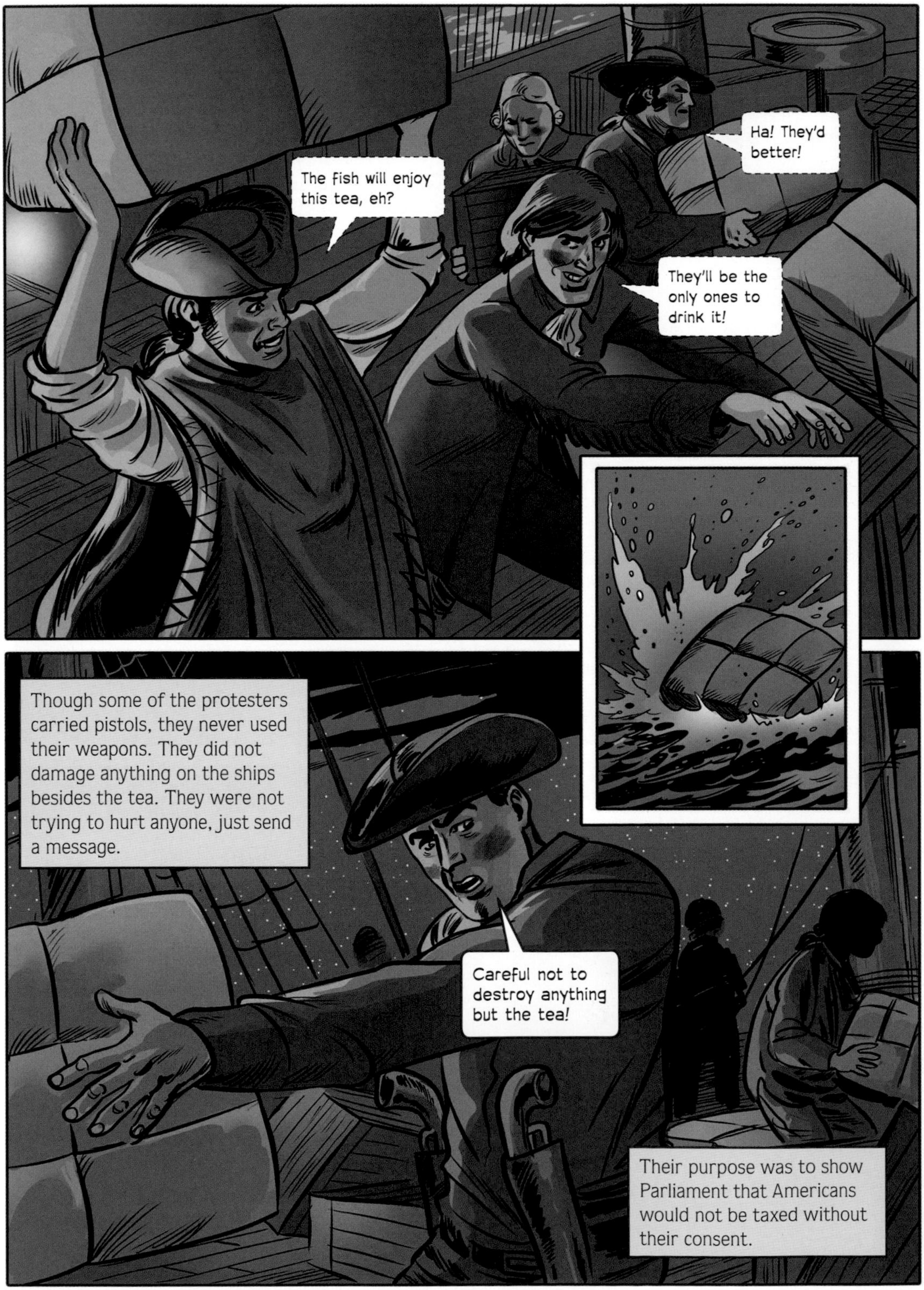
The fish will enjoy this tea, eh?
Ha! They'd better!
They'll be the only ones to drink it!
Though some of the protesters carried pistols, they never used their weapons. They did not damage anything on the ships besides the tea. They were not trying to hurt anyone, just send a message.
Careful not to destroy anything but the tea!
Their purpose was to show Parliament that Americans would not be taxed without their consent.

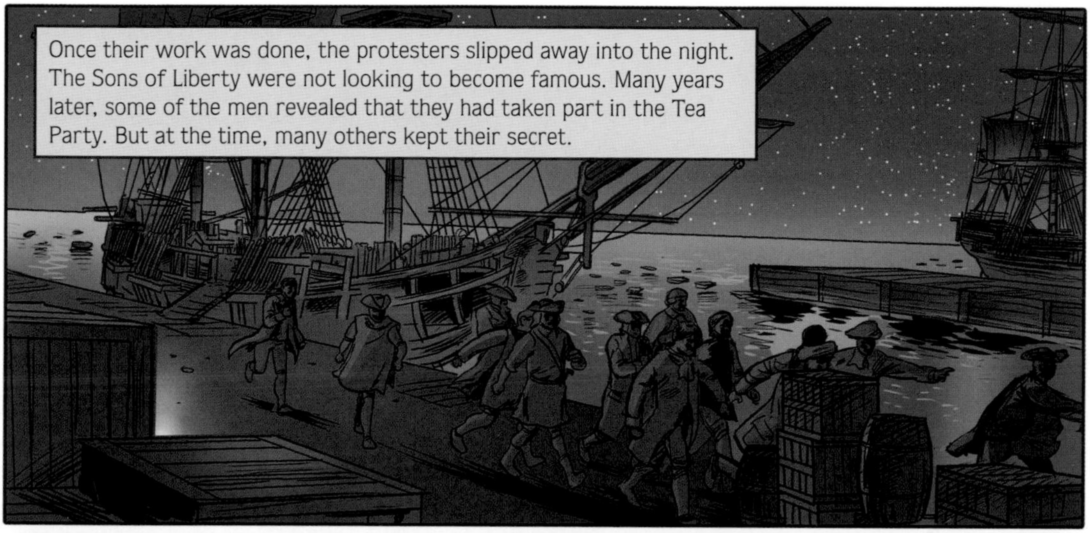
Once their work was done, the protesters slipped away into the night. The Sons of Liberty were not looking to become famous. Many years later, some of the men revealed that they had taken part in the Tea Party. But at the time, many others kept their secret.

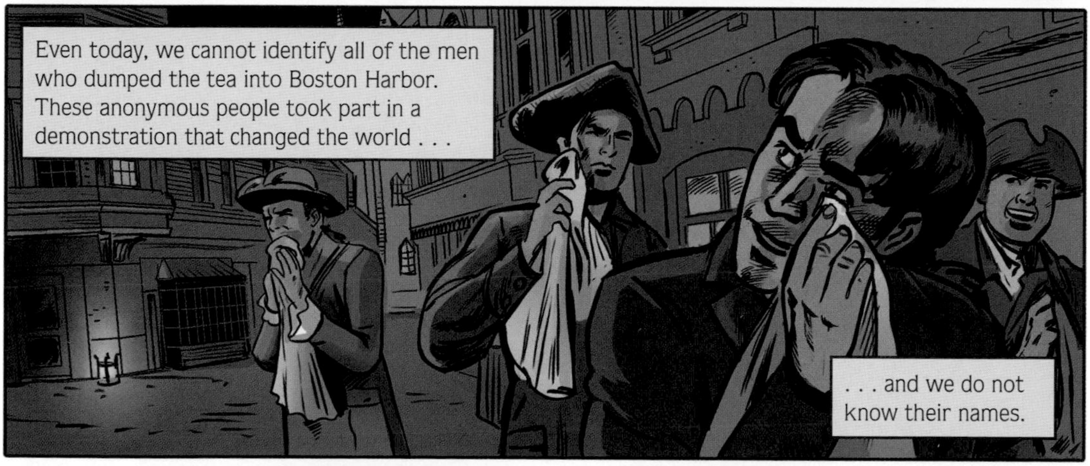
Even today, we cannot identify all of the men who dumped the tea into Boston Harbor. These anonymous people took part in a demonstration that changed the world . . .
. . . and we do not know their names.

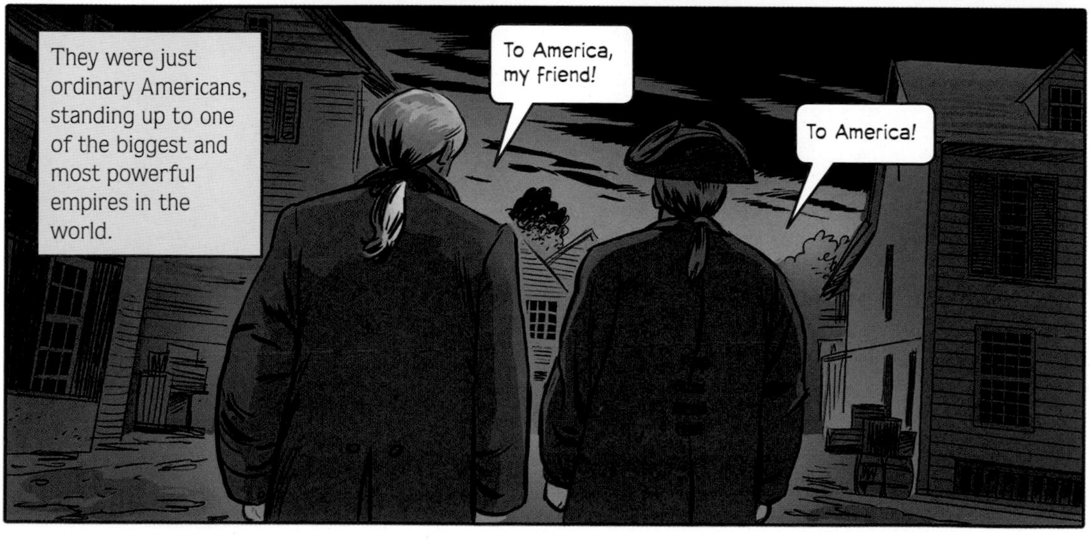
They were just ordinary Americans, standing up to one of the biggest and most powerful empires in the world.
To America, my friend!
To America!

AFTER THE TEA

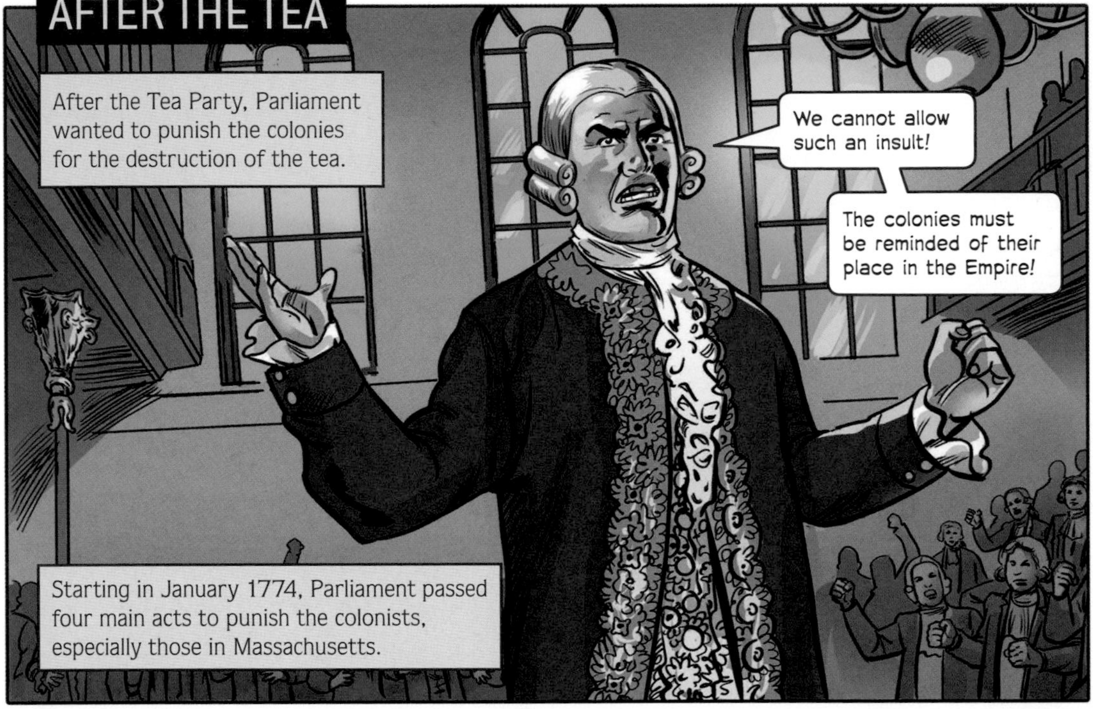
After the Tea Party, Parliament wanted to punish the colonies for the destruction of the tea.
We cannot allow such an insult!
The colonies must be reminded of their place in the Empire!
Starting in January 1774, Parliament passed four main acts to punish the colonists, especially those in Massachusetts.

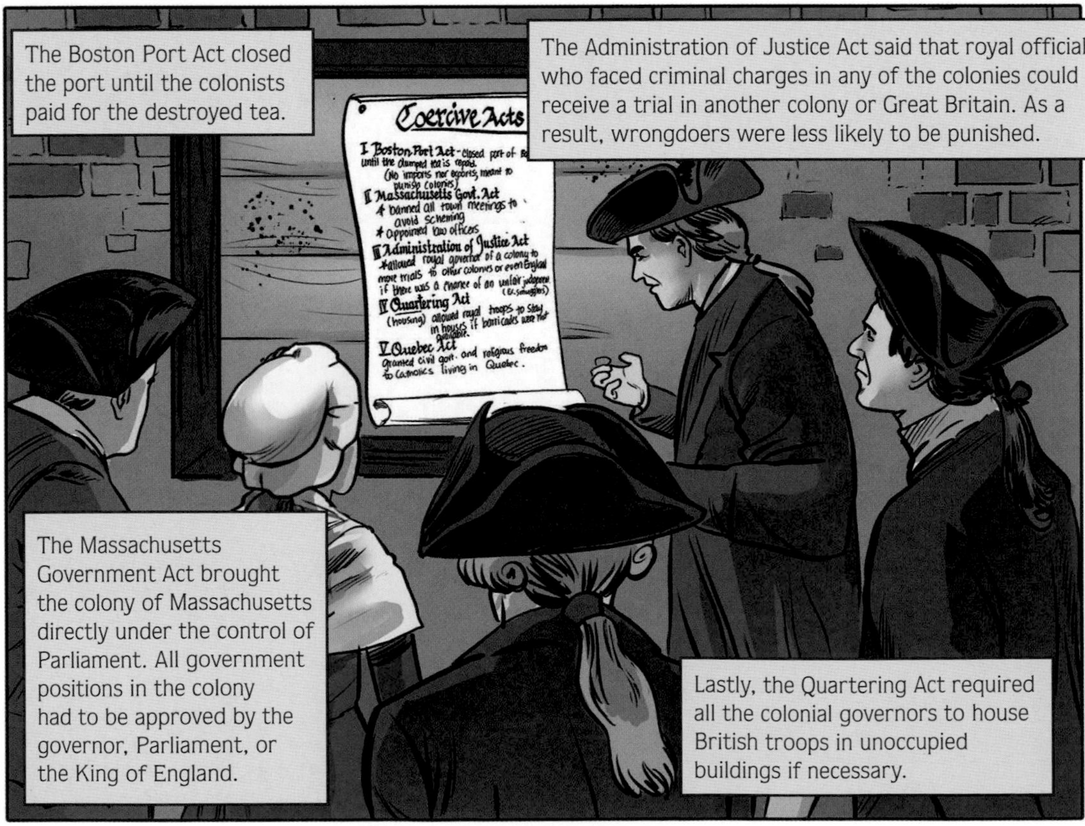
The Boston Port Act closed the port until the colonists paid for the destroyed tea.
Coercive Acts
I Boston Port Act - closed port of
until the dumped tea is repaid.
(No imports nor exports, meant to punish colonies)
II Massachusetts Govt. Act
* banned all town meetings to avoid scheming
* appointed law officers
III Administration of Justice Act
* allowed royal governor of a colony to move trials to other colonies or even England
IV Quartering Act
(housing)
V Quebec Act
granted civil govt. and religious freedom to Catholics living in Quebec.
The Administration of Justice Act said that royal officials who faced criminal charges in any of the colonies could receive a trial in another colony or Great Britain. As a result, wrongdoers were less likely to be punished.
The Massachusetts Government Act brought the colony of Massachusetts directly under the control of Parliament. All government positions in the colony had to be approved by the governor, Parliament, or the King of England.
Lastly, the Quartering Act required all the colonial governors to house British troops in unoccupied buildings if necessary.

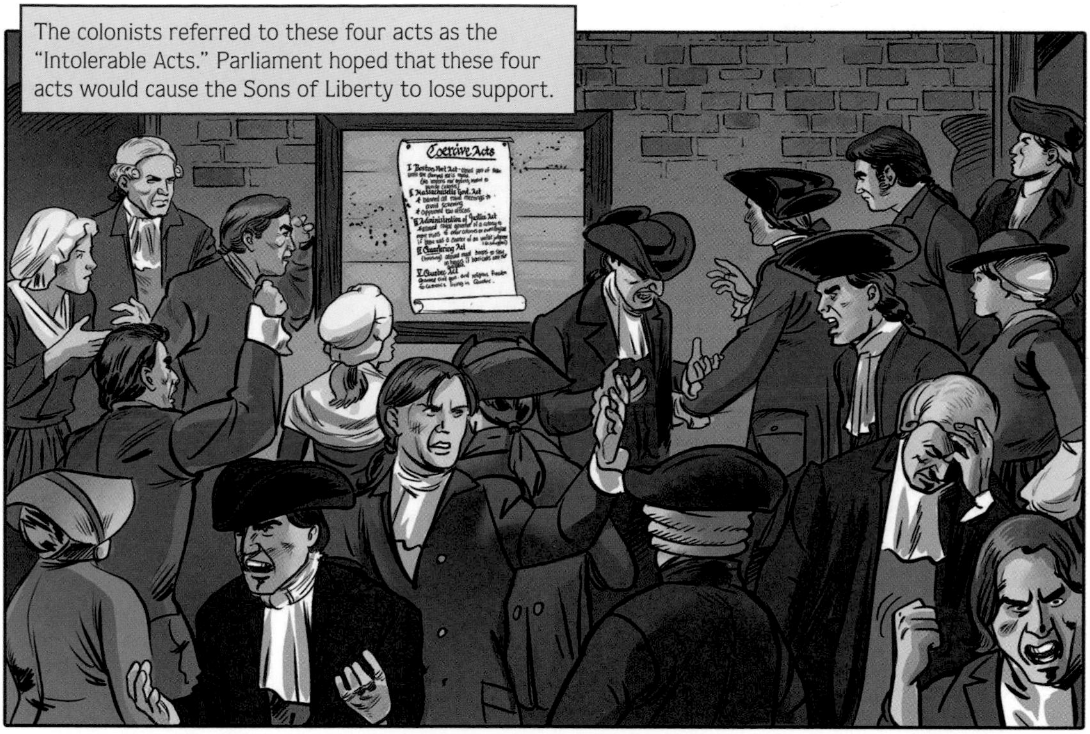
The colonists referred to these four acts as the "Intolerable Acts." Parliament hoped that these four acts would cause the Sons of Liberty to lose support.
Coercive Acts

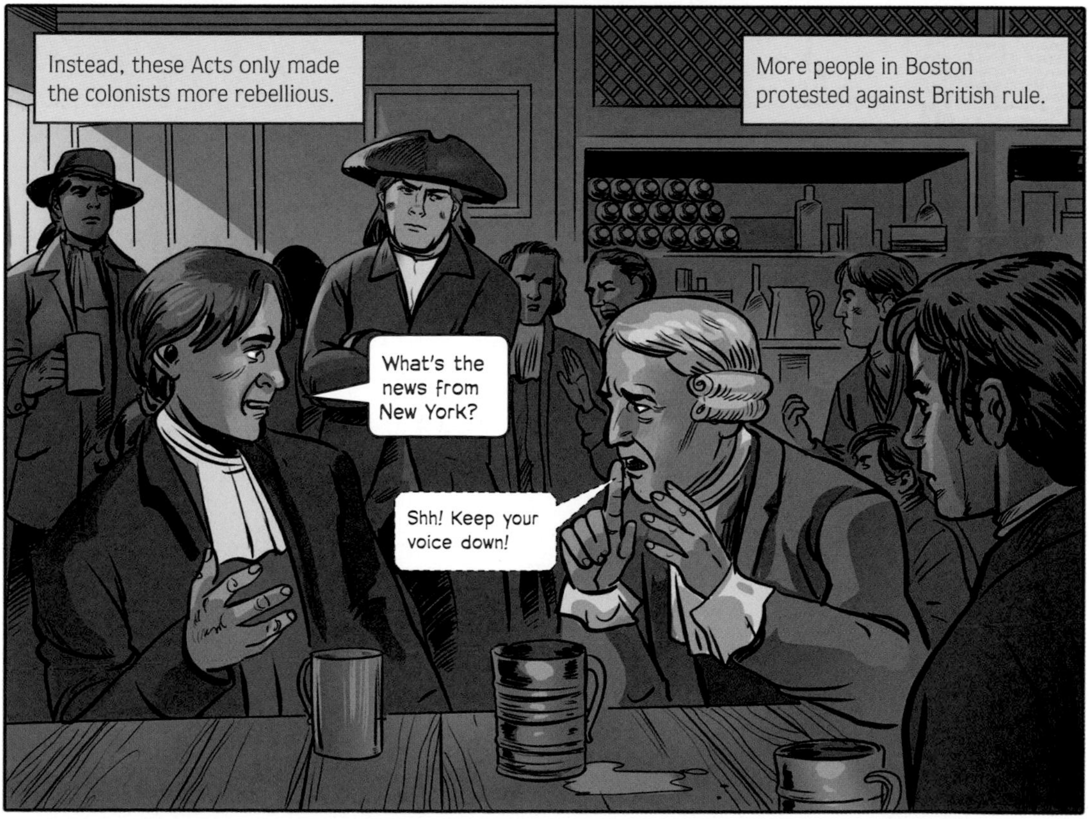
Instead, these Acts only made the colonists more rebellious.
More people in Boston protested against British rule.
What's the news from New York?
Shh! Keep your voice down!

COMMITTEES AND CONGRESS

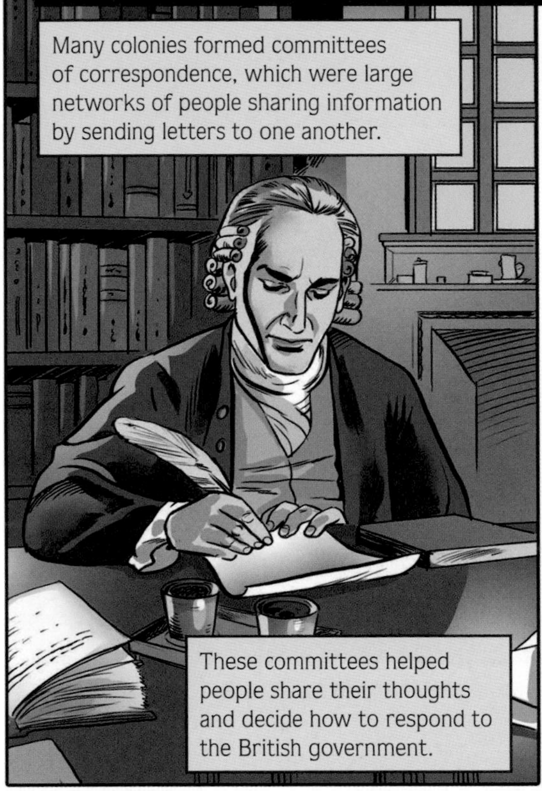
Many colonies formed committees of correspondence, which were large networks of people sharing information by sending letters to one another.
These committees helped people share their thoughts and decide how to respond to the British government.

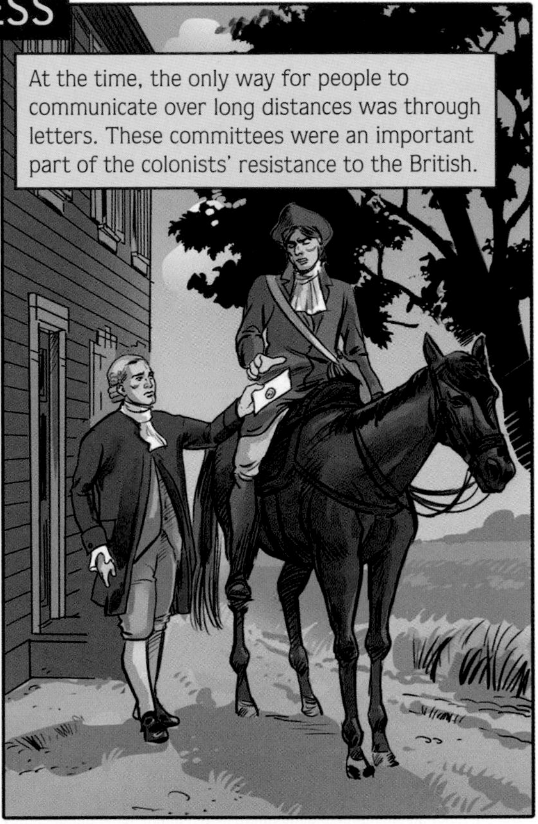
At the time, the only way for people to communicate over long distances was through letters. These committees were an important part of the colonists' resistance to the British.

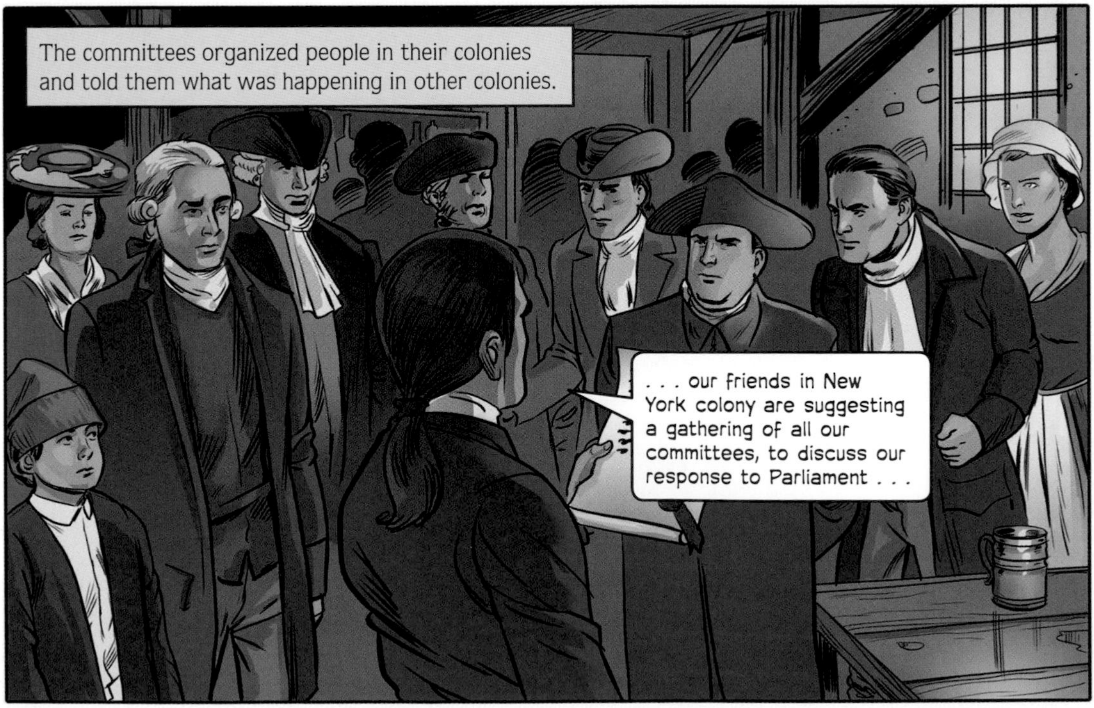
The committees organized people in their colonies and told them what was happening in other colonies.
. . . our friends in New York colony are suggesting a gathering of all our committees, to discuss our response to Parliament . . .

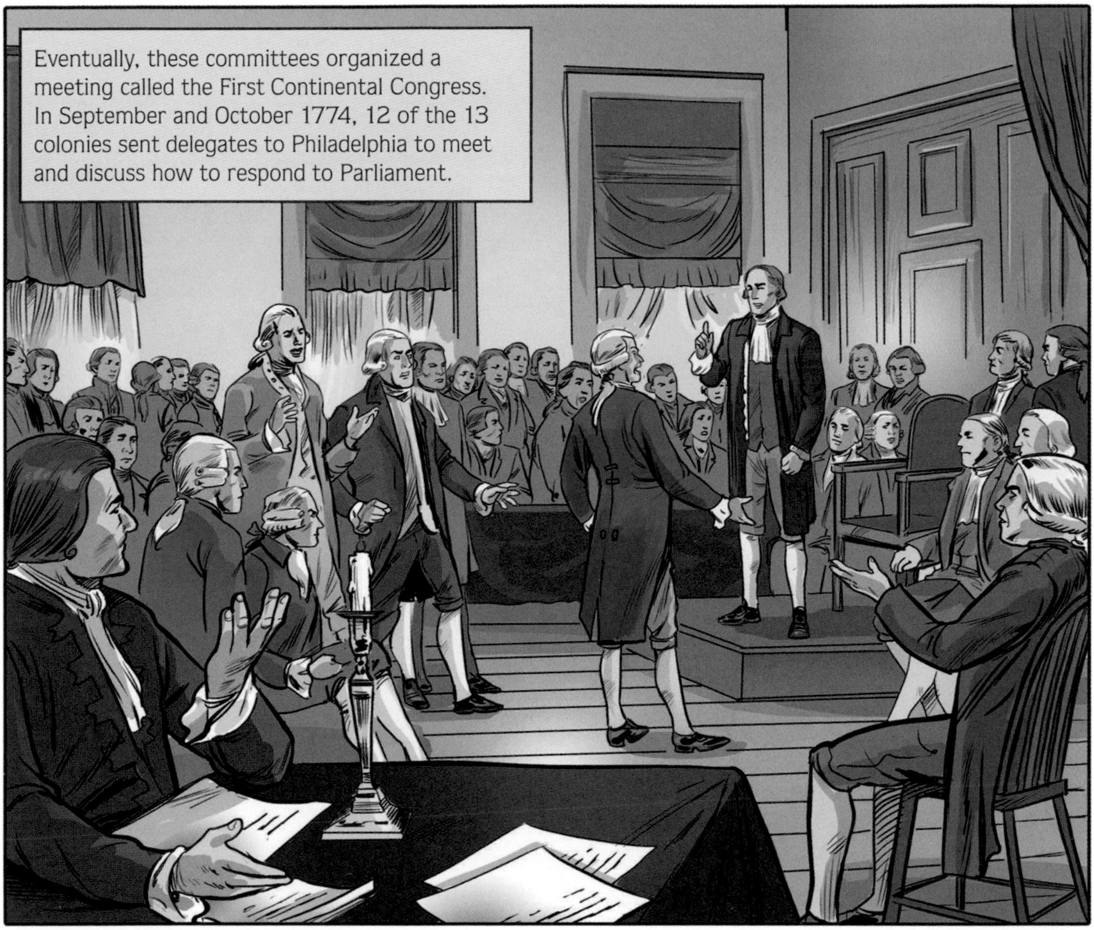
Eventually, these committees organized a meeting called the First Continental Congress. In September and October 1774, 12 of the 13 colonies sent delegates to Philadelphia to meet and discuss how to respond to Parliament.

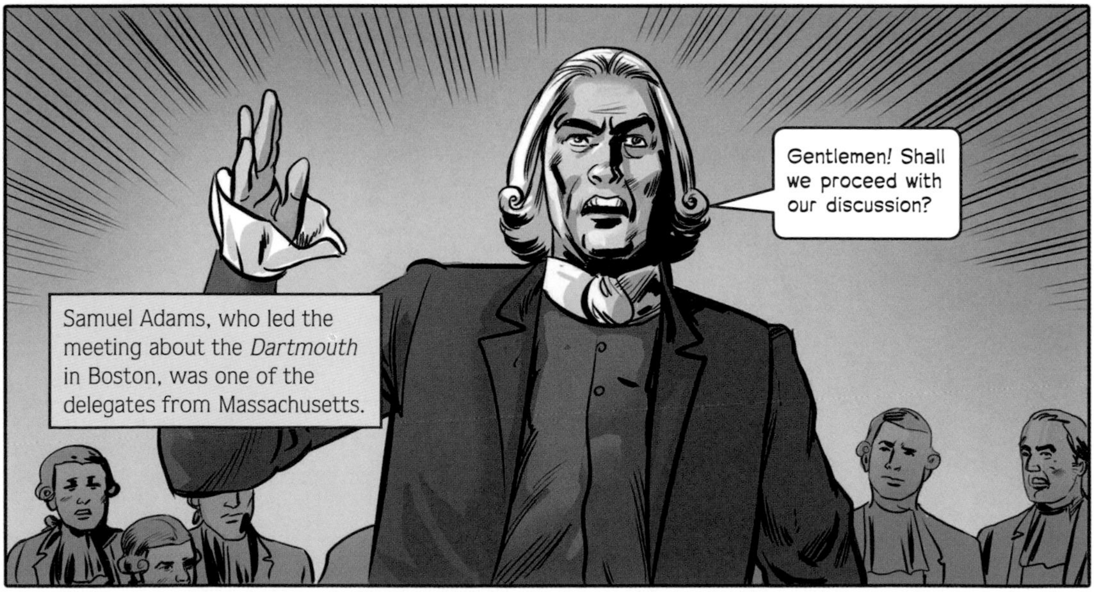
Gentlemen! Shall we proceed with our discussion?
Samuel Adams, who led the meeting about the *Dartmouth* in Boston, was one of the delegates from Massachusetts.

RUMBLINGS OF REBELLION

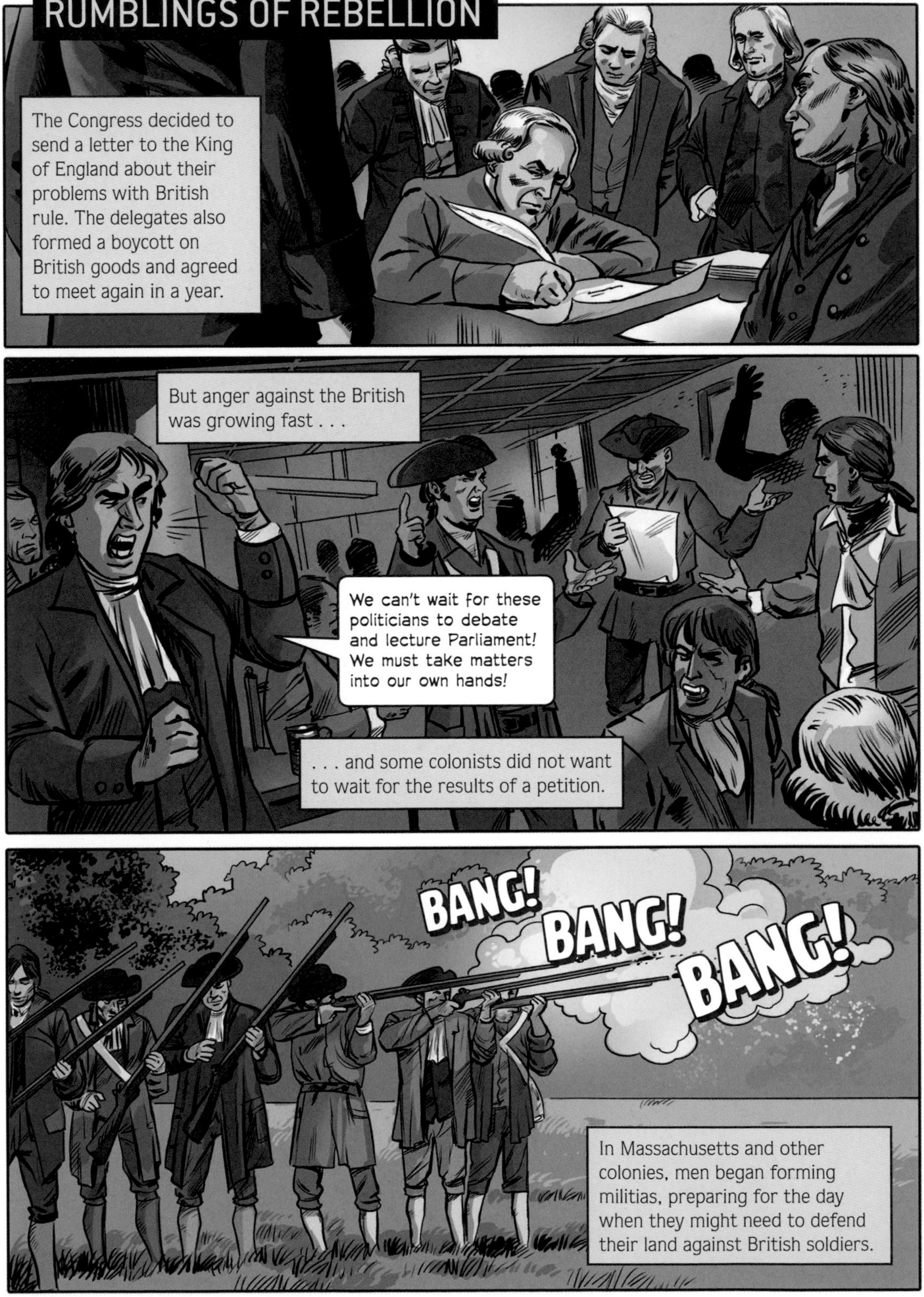
The Congress decided to send a letter to the King of England about their problems with British rule. The delegates also formed a boycott on British goods and agreed to meet again in a year.
But anger against the British was growing fast . . .
We can't wait for these politicians to debate and lecture Parliament! We must take matters into our own hands!
. . . and some colonists did not want to wait for the results of a petition.
BANG!
BANG!
BANG!
In Massachusetts and other colonies, men began forming militias, preparing for the day when they might need to defend their land against British soldiers.

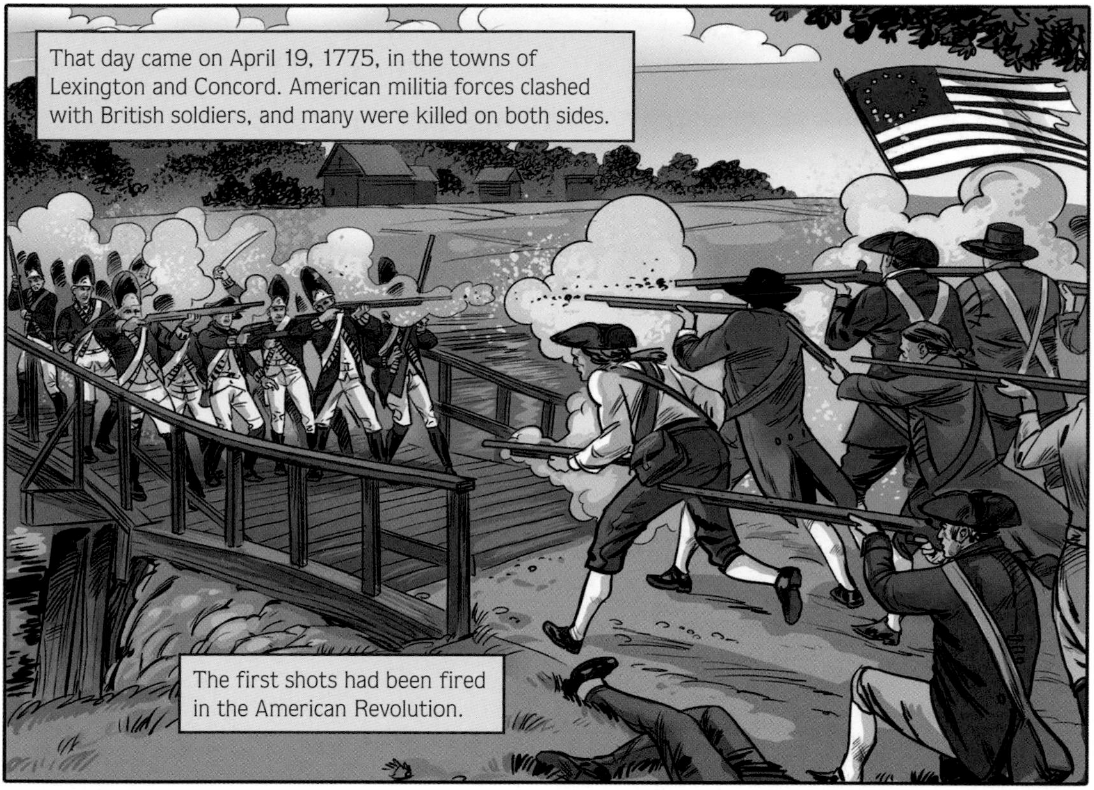
That day came on April 19, 1775, in the towns of Lexington and Concord. American militia forces clashed with British soldiers, and many were killed on both sides.
The first shots had been fired in the American Revolution.

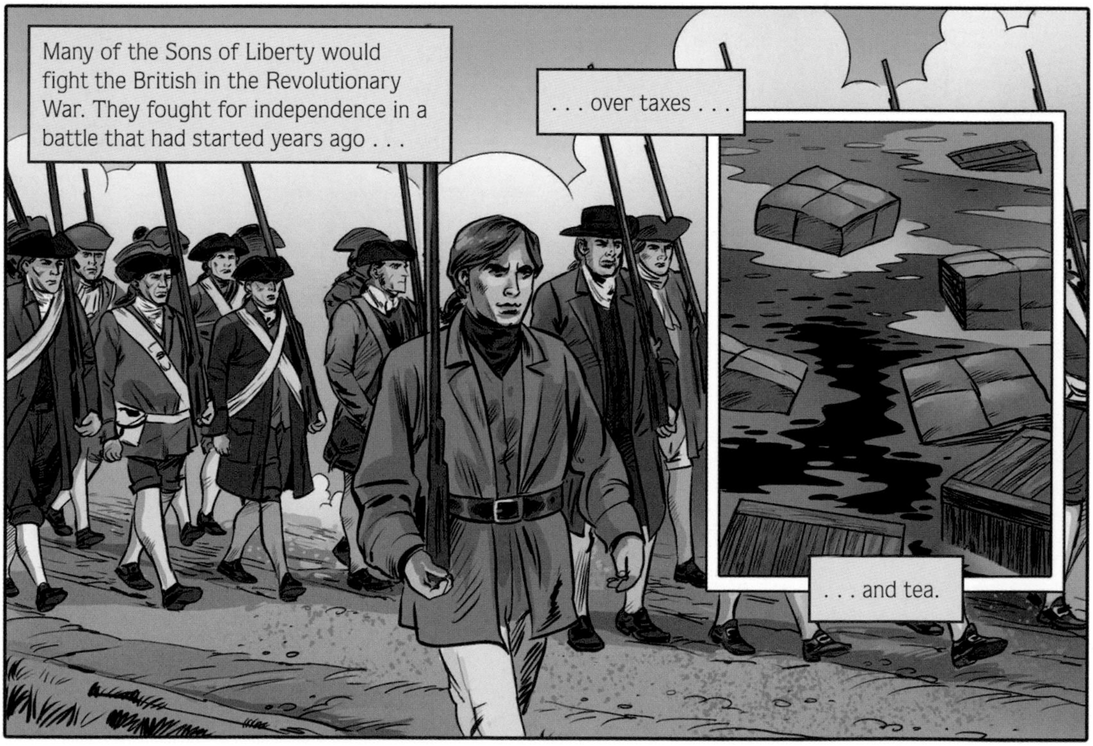
Many of the Sons of Liberty would fight the British in the Revolutionary War. They fought for independence in a battle that had started years ago . . .
. . . over taxes . . .
. . . and tea.

MORE ABOUT
THE TEA PARTY

The Boston Tea Party was not carried out by one individual, but by a group of men from many different walks of life. We should not forget that this event, and others like it, were carried out by ordinary people, working together for change.

Many thousands of men and women participated in the American Revolutionary War and won independence for America from the British Empire. But not all of these people had the same reasons for supporting the cause.

The Sons of Liberty, who carried out the Boston Tea Party, were mostly merchants, doctors, businessmen, and lawyers. Some of the Sons may have wanted independence because they believed in the ideals of liberty and democracy. Some may have simply disliked being controlled by the British.

While the Sons of Liberty was a group for men only, women formed a group called the Daughters of Liberty. This organization assisted with many protests. For example, it helped boycott British goods and wove cloth at home so they did not have to buy British fabric. But as far as we know, no women participated in the destruction of tea.

People at the time had different reactions to the Boston Tea Party. John Adams, a future president of the United States, was supportive of the protest. He wrote in his diary the day after the Tea Party, "This is the most magnificent Movement of all." However, George Washington wrote in June 1774 that he disapproved of "their conduct in destroying the tea." Benjamin Franklin, who was in England when the news about the Tea Party arrived, called it "an act of violent injustice on our part." Franklin had hoped to reduce tensions between England and America.

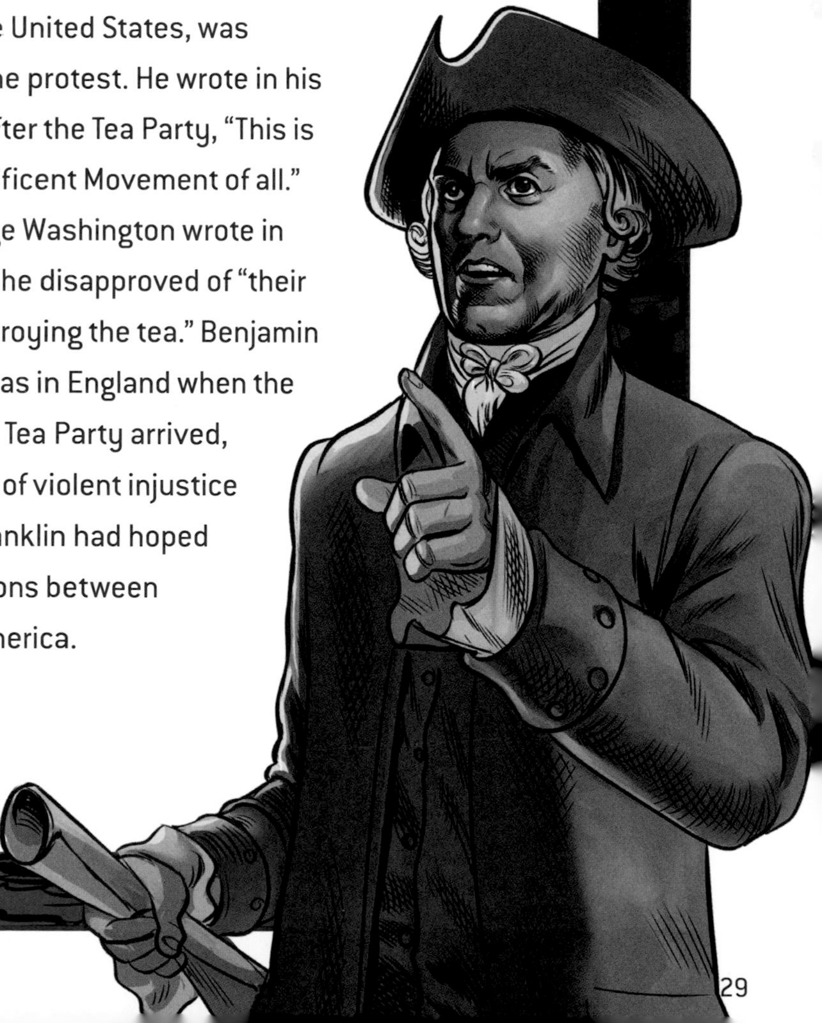

GLOSSARY

anonymous (uh-NON-uh-muhss)—written, done, or given by a person whose name is not known or made public

boycott (BOY-kot)—to stop buying something to show support for an idea or group of people

consent (kuhn-SENT)—willingly agreeing or saying yes

delegate (DEL-uh-guht)—a person who represents a larger group of people at a meeting

intolerable (in-TOL-ur-uh-buhl)—difficult to endure

legislature (LEJ-iss-lay-chur)—a group of elected officials who have the power to make or change laws

militia (muh-LISH-uh)—a group of volunteer citizens organized to fight, but who are not professional soldiers

monopoly (muh-NOP-uh-lee)—situation in which there is only one supplier of a good or service, and therefore that supplier can control the price

repeal (ri-PEEL)—to officially cancel something

revenue (REV-uh-noo)—money that a country gets from taxes and trade

smuggler (SMUHG-lur)—a person who sneaks illegal goods into or out of a country

tyranny (TIHR-uh-nee)—a cruel or unfair government in which all power is in the hands of a single ruler

wharf (WORF)—a man-made place for ships to dock

READ MORE

Cook, Peter. *You Wouldn't Want to Be at the Boston Tea Party!* New York: Franklin Watts, 2014.

Gilman, Sarah. *The Boston Tea Party.* New York: Enslow Publishing, 2016.

Krull, Kathleen. *What Was the Boston Tea Party?* New York: Grosset & Dunlap, 2013.

INTERNET SITES

Boston Tea Party Historical Society
http://www.boston-tea-party.org/

Boston Tea Party Ships & Museum
https://www.bostonteapartyship.com/

Old South Meeting House
http://www.oldsouthmeetinghouse.org/

INDEX